for John E. Oden and *White Collar Boxing*

"Don't let the white collar fool you. When he puts on the gloves and steps into the ring, John Oden is a fighter."

—TOMMY GALLAGHER, TRAINER, GYM OWNER
AND CO-STAR OF *THE CONTENDER*

"Boxing is a perfect metaphor for life and work in New York; demanding, exhausting, unforgiving but ultimately a source of great challenge, reward, and growth. *White Collar Boxing* is a great read for anyone who shares or seeks to better understand this story of the New York ethos."

—G. DAVID BEDNAR, INVESTMENT BANKER, GOLDMAN SACHS

"John Oden's book is extraordinary. He is lyrical in his description of the agony and exultation that accompanies the pugilist's life. The book is a great read."

—JOHN V. TUNNEY, FORMER U.S. SENATOR
AND SON OF GENE TUNNEY,
FORMER HEAVYWEIGHT CHAMPION OF THE WORLD

"John E. Oden is a great student of the game, a quick study with good punching power, and a terrific ambassador for white collar boxing."

—GERRY COONEY, FORMER #1 WORLD HEAVYWEIGHT
CONTENDER AND FOUNDER OF F.I.S.T.

"If I had more fighters that had the same passion for boxing as John Oden, my company would be the promoter of more World Champions. Everything John does is 110%."

—CEDRIC KUSHNER, INTERNATIONAL BOXING PROMOTER

"As a fellow white-collar boxer (I was on the card with John at Hedge Fund Fight Night in London in 2004), I can confirm everything that John has so dynamically characterized in this book. This book does an outstanding job of describing what boxing does to a man, both physically and mentally, the importance of pride in one's accomplishments, the ability to withstand and work through pain, and how it prepares one for life's daily bouts. John's crusade to become a boxer is one that will likely become a white-collar boxing legend. Don't miss it!"

—JUSTIN DEW, SENIOR HEDGE FUND SPECIALIST,
STANDARD & POOR'S

"Just when you thought everything about boxing had been written, along comes this magnificent book by John Oden, giving us a different view from a different pew, one as seen through the eyes of the white-collar boxer. *White Collar Boxing* is deserving of a place on all boxing—no, make that all sports—fans' bookshelves."

—BERT RANDOLPH SUGAR, BOXING HALL OF FAME WRITER

"I've known John Oden for more than forty years—from the lean years in a small Texas town to his business successes in New York—he's been a fighter all the way. As this book shows, in the ring or out, John's a champion."

—D. EDWARD MARTIN, PARTNER, EISNER LLC

"John E. Oden and his great book, *White Collar Boxing*, becomes our 'evangelical ambassador' for the genre of white collar boxing because he spreads the good word on boxing and its redemptive features. He also is our uncrowned white collar heavyweight world champion."

—PETROS AND NIKOS SPANAKOS, AMATEUR BOXING CHAMPIONS

"John Oden is not only a boxing devotee, his enthusiasm for the game is further manifested through his ability to leverage its popularity for worthwhile causes. Through his tireless efforts with F.I.S.T. (Fighters' Initiative for Support and Training), John uses his left / right combination to raise awareness of the athletes the sweet science has left behind. Through John's charitable and professional initiatives, countless current and former pugilists have a renewed sense of dignity."

—PAUL A. WATERS, SENIOR VICE PRESIDENT,
THE STAUBACH COMPANY

"John Oden has captured the unique essence of the sport of boxing. This unlikely warrior conveys the discipline, dedication and courage required for success in the 'sweet science.' Using the sport as a vehicle for public service, he has also dedicated himself most impressively to raising funds for great New York charities. It's enough to give boxing a good name!"

—STEVE CROSSON, CHAIRMAN AND CEO OF
CROSSON DANNIS, INC., SPECIAL ADVISOR TO THE PRESIDENT
AND FORMER WORLD CLASS REFEREE, WORLD BOXING COUNCIL

"If you sometimes feel you're 'fighting' your way through a day, you might want to pick up *White Collar Boxing*, a book written by businessman John E. Oden, and before you know it, you'll be bobbing and weaving to a win!"

—TEDDY ATLAS, WORLD-CLASS TRAINER
AND FAMED BOXING COMMENTATOR

"As an artist and an athlete, and a boxer with many championships, I was fascinated with this new book by John Oden on white collar boxing. Cover to cover, I don't think there could be a more complete presentation of white collar boxing than this wonderful book, which John has written from his own experiences and which provides the reader with everything they might want to know about this unique subset of the sweet science."
—JACK KENDRICK, IRISH COLLEGIATE BOXING CHAMPION
AND U.S. ARMY BOXING CHAMPION

"If you have a passion and it happens to be boxing, then you need to read this gentleman's perspective. *White Collar Boxing* is a knockout!"
—JEFF MESHEL, PRESIDENT OF MERCURY CAPITAL CORPORATION
AND AUTHOR OF *ONE PHONE CALL AWAY*

"Captivating. Heavy hitting. An authentic boxing story that I couldn't put down. Oden has stepped into the ring with a powerful one-two combination of courage and commitment that will inspire readers of all ages to live their dreams. I recommend this book highly."
—DON KING, LEGENDARY BOXING PROMOTER

"John Oden has joined the ranks of Teddy Roosevelt and Nelson Mandela as gentlemen-boxers who excel in life and the ring. *White Collar Boxing* is an exciting trip into boxing history and into the life of one individual who has fulfilled the dream (that so many of us have) of being a participant and not just a spectator in this sweetest of sweet sciences."
—JOHN W. ALLEN, CHAIRMAN AND CEO,
GREATER CHINA CORPORATION

"John's story of 'boxing' through life was riveting, cover to cover. The rich friendships and personal fulfillment that getting in the ring has brought to John during his mid-life years is a great story very well told."

—ARTHUR J. MAHON, COUNSEL, MCDERMOTT WILL & EMERY

"White collar, blue collar, or no collar when you're in the fray—mental and physical capabilities, skills, courage, and character are required in the ring just as in the rest of life. John Oden brings them all to bear in his life and in the book he has written."

—TOM GIMBEL, HEDGE FUND INVESTMENT MANAGER AND
CHAMPION WHITE COLLAR BOXER

"White men CAN box!!! Watch this white boy go!!!"

—GENE SIMMONS, KISS

"I have had the privilege to work with John for three years. I have witnessed firsthand how his unwavering commitment, perseverance, and strong character have contributed to his success both in the business world and in the ring. John embodies the perception of 'The Man Who Thinks He Can.' This book is not only a window into the intriguing world of white collar boxing, but a superb example of how to set forth a series of goals and actually attain them. This book is a must read for any college graduate seeking wisdom and advice on how to succeed in this increasingly competitive marketplace. Thank you, John, for being the consummate example of a competitor and a professional."

—DANIEL N. ROMANOW, SENIOR ASSOCIATE TO JOHN E. ODEN,
BERNSTEIN INVESTMENT RESEARCH AND MANAGEMENT

Brandon Sim

WHITE COLLAR BOXING

One Man's Journey
from the Office to the Ring

JOHN E. ODEN

"The Pecos Kid"

HATHERLEIGH PRESS
NEW YORK • LONDON

Hatherleigh Press
5-22 46th Avenue, Suite 200
Long Island City, NY 11101
www.hatherleighpress.com

Oden, John E
White Collar Boxing : One Man's Journey from the Office to the
Ring / John E. Oden.
p. cm.
Includes bibliographical references.
ISBN 1-57826-207-0
1. Oden, John E. 2. Boxers (Sports)—United States—Biography.
3. Boxing—United States. I. Title.
GV1132.O34A3 2005
796.83'0973—dc22
2005021998

ISBN 1-57826-207-0
White Collar Boxing is available for bulk purchase, special
promotions, and premiums. For information on reselling and
special purchase opportunities, call 800-528-2550 and ask for the
Special Sales Manager.

Interior design by Deborah Miller, Jacinta Monniere
Cover design by Deborah Miller, Phil Mondestin

Front cover photograph by John Gichigi/Getty Images
Back cover photographs by Richard Price

10 9 8 7 6 5 4 3 2 1
Printed in Canada

To Violet, my inspiration and biggest fan

Life is a balance between the necessity of hard work,
and finding time for family and relaxation.
To master life is to master the balance.

—MARI MONAHAN

WHITE
COLLAR
BOXING

Contents

PREFACE

I remember watching a television program once on the career of George Foreman. This was back in the 1980s, when George was between his "first" career as a young, fierce, silent, larger-than-life terror in the ring, and his "second" career, as an older, bald, friendlier, cuddlier, family-man-returned-to-pugilist. (He became Heavyweight Champion of the World in both careers.) George was quite introspective on the program, and discussed the finite number of years during which one could expect to pursue a boxing career. He was working as a minister in Houston at this time, and had not yet announced his return to the ring. One of the great lines I remember from the program was "At a certain point in a man's life, he looks ridiculous running down a road." This, of course, was a reference to all of the road work, or running (often done on roads or streets), necessary for a boxer to train for the endurance needed to fight. It also meant that certain sports and athletic endeavors, such as boxing, should be reserved for the young. Those words had a big impact on me at the time, as they reminded me of my own mortality. I was still in my thirties and not a boxer at the time; but I had always thought about taking up the sport, and was not happy to consider that perhaps my dream was out of reach.

Of course, George Foreman made a comeback to boxing when he was in his forties, once again reclaiming the heavyweight championship of the world. In fact, he fought throughout his forties and into his fifties, and he looked great doing it! He has been an inspiration to any observer of the sport. Along the way, he achieved great fame and fortune. As George and I are about the same age, I watched his journey with great interest and admiration.

George Foreman's achievements had reinforced one of my greatest beliefs: Boxing is a sport that can be practiced by anyone, regardless of age, background, physical condition, handicap or disability. It is the *best* form of exercise, and can be a fabulous way to form great friendships and have fun. Although George appears to have retired for a second time, there is an occasional rumor of his making a third comeback to the ring. So I am sure that, today, George Foreman would be the first to acknowledge that a man can look just fine running down a road at any age. Or he can *box*!

At the root of everything that people do, or accomplish, is an idea. The world, however, is full of people with ideas, and short on those who can bring them to fruition. This is true in business, personal relationships, and certainly, athletic endeavors. I always admired the late George Plimpton, a Harvard-trained aristocrat, who took up several sports for short periods of time, training at the highest professional levels, and wrote about his experiences. To pursue his literary and athletic interests, Plimpton boxed with Archie Moore, pitched to Willie Mays, and trained with the Detroit Lions football team. He even performed as a trapeze artist for the Clyde Beatty-Cole Brothers Circus. What Mr. Plimpton proved to himself, and to others who saw him perform, is that the average fan, or outsider, had little place on the playing field with great professional athletes. Nevertheless, I always admired his courage to jump in the ring, or the game (in the case of baseball or football), and give it a try. As I reached adulthood, and realized that the outlet for my athletic interests seemed somewhat limited, I always wondered if there might be some middle ground for me to pursue a sport on a competitive level that would allow me to enjoy boxing, or other intensively competitive sports normally reserved for the professional ranks, much as Mr. Plimpton had done.

White collar boxing bridged the gap for me. Without taking undue risks or putting me in situations that might prove to be overly embarrassing, it gave me the platform to pursue and compete in an intense sport under a highly supervised and instructional backdrop. I have been able to compete with people just like me, businessmen and others who want to get in shape and enjoy good competition at a demanding sport. And after almost 14 years of boxing, I'm still going strong, probably in the best shape of my life. I greatly admire both George Foreman and George Plimpton, who served as a great inspiration to me, but they both had special skill sets which the average person probably can not duplicate. The path I have chosen can be pursued by anyone, as I hope my story will demonstrate.

CHAPTER 1

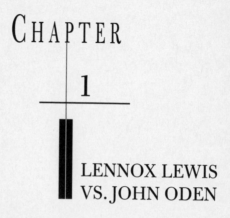

LENNOX LEWIS VS. JOHN ODEN

A man's reach should exceed his grasp. . . .
—ROBERT BROWNING, ENGLISH POET

In the year 2000, the great professional World Heavyweight Champion, Lennox Lewis, fought three times, successfully defending his title in each fight. He fought a total of 16 rounds. First, in April of that year, he triumphed over Michael Grant in New York City with a knockout (KO) in the second round. Then, in London in July, he KO'd Francis Botha in the second round. Finally, in Las Vegas in October, he won a 12-round decision over David Tua. These were three great fights against three of the top contenders of the day, so it can truly be said that Lennox Lewis had a very good year in 2000. He also made a bundle of money.

In that same year, I fought five times as a journeyman "white collar boxer." All of my fights were three two-minute rounds, and they all went the distance with no knockouts, for a total of 15 rounds. So, that year, I fought 15 rounds versus Lennox at 16 rounds, and five fights versus Lennox who fought three. Only one of my fights was a competitive bout with a declared winner—the club championship in May at the New York Athletic Club, in which I won a three-round decision in the heavyweight division over Mark Settembre. The fight with Mark had been a particularly challenging one, as we fought the last heavyweight bout of the evening in the club's massive gymnasium in front of a large crowd. He was a strong, physically imposing guy with massive arms. My friends told me later that they were nervous for me when they saw how big he was. But apparently Mark was nervous, too; he had some trouble with his footing in the first round and I was able to control the fight by keeping my jab in his face. This, along with some good defensive skills, helped me win the decision.

My other four fights were white collar bouts, in which there was no declared winner or loser, and both participants received a trophy. Of the four remaining fights, one was in London in July, as was the second of Lennox's fights in 2000, which took place the same week as mine. In the London bout, I was a member of the white collar team assembled by Gleason's Gym to represent the USA against a British white collar team sponsored by Alan Lacey and The Real Fight Club, a London-based white collar boxing promotion company. Another was at Gleason's against Alan Lacey's British team, when they came to New York for a rematch in November. The final two of my five fights were "white collar sparring" nights at Gleason's Gym, one in June and one in July of that year. Unfortunately, unlike Lennox Lewis, I made no money by boxing that year, since I am not a professional boxer. I have a professional career that includes a good, paying position with a global money management firm, and I don't participate in the sport to make money.

Without a doubt, any professional boxer faces a huge emotional challenge when he or she enters the ring. I am certain that Lennox Lewis, who faced such boxing talent as Michael Grant, Francis Botha, and David Tua, had many an unsettling moment as he prepared for these fights and then came face to face with his opponents. Despite his excellent skills as a boxer, the pressure must have been intense. This is boxing at its absolute highest level. Lennox Lewis undoubtedly had to draw on every resource within himself to train into superb physical and mental condition, so that he could perform at the top of his game. No doubt this training included a strict diet, great physical discipline and exercise, regular hours of sleep, and intense concentration on his goals. This kind of sacrifice, very common in the sport of boxing, is also accompanied by periods of isolation, during which a fighter feels as though he is truly alone as he journeys down the road ahead of him. Though boxing is a sport that can draw large crowds in huge arenas, the boxer's journey is a solitary one, in which he must depend heavily on his own inner resources to motivate himself for the long hours of grueling training and disciplined living. This culminates in the moment when he stands alone in a ring and faces his opponent, an opponent whose intentions are usually to "take his head off."

I know the roots of all of these feelings experienced by Lennox Lewis or any other professional boxer, because, you see, I am a "white collar boxer." I am in my mid-fifties, and do this sport for fun, exercise, and because it gives me a level of exhilaration that nothing else can. I've tried football, baseball, tennis, golf, running, handball, racquetball, basketball, and a barrage of other worthy, challenging sports. In fact, I did not take up boxing until I was in my early forties, a time when most professional boxers have long since retired. Lennox Lewis was 38 when he retired in 2003.

Today, boxing has three distinct categories of participation. The first is professional boxing, represented by the Oscar de la Hoya's and the Lennox Lewis's of the world—pros who fight for money. Fights can be staged for up to 12 three-minute rounds, with one minute between rounds. Eight-ounce gloves are used.

The second category is amateur. There are two major formal organizations that exist at the amateur level, the Olympics and the Golden Gloves. In addition, certain other groups, such as the police departments and fire departments of large cities, have organized teams that compete all over the world. Both professional and amateur boxing matches are always fought on a competitive level, with a winner and loser declared at the end of each fight.

USA Boxing, as the national governing body for Olympic-style boxing, is the United States' member organization of the International Amateur Boxing Association (AIBA). Boxing first appeared at the Olympic Games in 1904, and, apart from the Games of 1912, has always been part of them. As a national governing body, USA Boxing is responsible for the administration, development, and promotion of Olympic-style boxing in the United States. In addition to developing the sport and its athletes at the local, regional, and national levels, it sponsors national and international dual competitions and selects teams for international events, including the Olympic Games, World Championships, and the Pan American Games. Formerly known as the United States Amateur Boxing Federation, USA Boxing has governed men's amateur boxing in the United States since 1988. Although women's boxing made an appearance as a demonstration bout at the Olympic Games of 1904, it has yet to reappear. However, as I will describe later, women's amateur boxing has made great strides in recent years.

Amateur boxing is usually three or four two-minute rounds, with one minute between rounds. Twelve-ounce gloves are used. Olympic and Golden Gloves boxers must be under 35 years of age. There is also a Master's Boxing group for fighters 35 years of age and over, which is administered by USA Boxing. Master's Boxing matches are three two-minute rounds, with one minute between rounds. Fighters who choose to participate in the Master's Boxing program of USA

Boxing must regularly demonstrate that they are fit and able to compete, by means of completing a physical fitness examination administered at specified intervals.

The Golden Gloves is an organization of thirty franchise units spanning from New England to Hawaii, representing every section of the country. Dating back to 1923, the Golden Gloves organization sponsors local, regional, and national tournaments which allow young aspiring boxers between the ages of 8 and 34 to compete and challenge themselves. More than 22,000 male and female athletes participate in Golden Gloves competitions each year. Many former Golden Gloves champions have gone on to become world champions, such as Joe Louis (1934), Muhammad Ali (1960), Sugar Ray Leonard (1973), Evander Holyfield (1984), and Oscar De La Hoya (1989).

The third category of boxers are the white collar boxers, guys like me who are businessmen, attorneys, accountants, doctors, office workers, policemen—"regular guys" who love the sport and use it to get into great shape and have fun. Today this activity is known as white collar boxing, since it is competitive but there is usually no winner or loser declared. White collar boxing can be found in athletic clubs, like the New York Athletic Club, and other private clubs around the country, and in certain boxing gyms throughout the world that promote competitive and white collar matches, like Gleason's Gym. No particular qualifications are set forth, as a rule, although many gyms, including Gleason's, require fighters to sign an acknowledgement that they are aware of the risks and will waive rights to bring legal action against the gym in the event of injury. In a very real sense, white collar boxing is less organized than the other two categories, and can be both competitive or noncompetitive, depending on the circumstances.

The terms "white collar boxing" and "white collar sparring" are used interchangeably to refer to this particular subset of non-professional, non-amateur boxing. Contests are staged in local gyms and clubs around the world, and consist of three two-minute rounds, with one minute between rounds. Sixteen-ounce gloves are used. Again, no winner or loser is declared, and both participants receive equal recognition at the end of a fight with both fighters' hands being raised. The first white collar boxing match was held at Gleason's Gym in Brooklyn in 1988 between Dr. David Lawrence, a successful Wall Street professional with a Ph.D. in English literature, and Dr. Richard Novack, an attorney/veterinarian. The card was completed with two other bouts, and a new boxing era had begun. Gleason's monthly White Collar Sparring nights are now legendary, with as many as 15 fights on a Friday night card and standing room only among the spectators, as up to 200 people crowd into the gym.

Bruce Silverglade, the owner of Gleason's Gym and the godfather of white collar boxing, maintains that natural ability doesn't make a winner at the sport. "The only person who can make a champ is the person himself . . . not the trainer, the manager, or anyone else. Boxing is 50 percent mental, 40 percent conditioning, and 10 percent ability." He also insists that behavior *outside the ring* separates those who will excel at the sport, from those who will not. "You need the smarts and discipline to be dedicated at all times when training at the sport, particularly when preparing for a match. You have to follow all of the instructions of your trainers, and concentrate on fundamentals and technique. Boxing has a *zone* which is all its own, and the mental part of the game plays a huge role in success at the sport." Thanks to individuals like Bruce, white collar boxing is alive and well in New York City, as well as in many other parts of the world, and gaining momentum with each passing day.

Nevertheless, boxing as a recreational sport for the average citizen is certainly not universally accepted. I have attended many a cocktail party or formal dinner where the fact that I am a boxer was eventually mentioned. A lot of people understand

and appreciate the sport. A lot of people do not. Those people often ask, "*Why* do you want to box?" The emphasis is usually on the word "why," and it is asked in a quizzical, even skeptical way. It is asked in a way that is meant to put me on the defensive, to make me feel I have to explain this ridiculous pastime of mine. For, you see, I am an investment professional on Wall Street, and also have many cultural and philanthropic interests. In addition to boxing, I like opera, music, the theater—I collect art and antiques. I sit on several philanthropic boards. So why, they say, would I ever want to do something that is so barbaric, so bloody, so hurtful to my opponent? Why would I, an ostensibly cultured and successful man, ever consider this sport when there are so many other ways to exercise and stay in shape? Why would I want to be associated with a sport in which men try to bite each other's ears off?

I have great patience for these questions. Every time I'm asked them, I calmly explain my love and passion for the sport of boxing. I tell them why I would rather be a white collar boxer than anything else, as far as athletics and physical fitness are concerned. I mention the exhilaration of a boxing workout, noting the terrific cardiovascular and aerobic benefits. I describe how boxing has not only helped me stay in great physical shape, but it has made my life more interesting and unique. It's a sport that can be performed at any age, without undue risk of harm or injury. I also mention that it takes less time than many sports, such as golf, and can be a more efficient way for a busy professional to get a good workout and stay in shape. For example, I can walk into the New York Athletic Club, which is five blocks from my office, at 6 P.M., have a great workout, and still make a business dinner at 8 P.M. the same evening. Contrast that to a round of golf, which takes a full morning or afternoon.

By the time I have finished my response, the person I'm addressing usually acknowledges that boxing might have more merit than they had originally thought. Frankly, I can understand the skepticism of some people when it comes to boxing. Admittedly, it's a rough sport, a heavy contact sport. And there is a "dark side" of boxing. By this I mean the "bad guy" image it conjures up. Images of ex-cons who take up the sport, people who attempt to bite each other's ears off, and the rumored "fixing" of fights come to mind. Unfortunately, a few bad apples have given boxing a black eye. People who judge any sport by one or two, or even ten, people who participate in it are not being fair. And the rules are not applied uniformly to all sports. Did baseball suffer when Pete Rose was banned from allegedly betting on games in the 1980s? Did basketball suffer because of the alleged sexual misconduct of Kobe Bryant? I could cite myriad instances of accused player violations, unsportsmanlike conduct, and unfair practices in professional sports over the years. But when it happens in boxing, it's headline news, and that's what people remember. Most boxers I know, however, are gentlemen and gracious athletes.

Here's the real point: I think of boxing as the quintessential sport, the sport to which all other sports should aspire. If you think of all sports as mock forms of combat, which they are in their most basic terms, then boxing is the ultimate sport. It pits two athletes in a small ring, with no one to rely on but themselves. There is no team. It is "you" versus "him" (or "her"). It is *mano a mano* in its purest form. There is no lonelier feeling in the world than when the referee says "seconds out" (meaning assistants and trainers are to leave the ring). It is the quintessential "moment of truth." And it is just as riveting and intense a moment for a white collar boxer, in my opinion, as a professional or amateur boxer.

Boxing has one characteristic that makes it completely different from anything I have ever done in athletics. It is the "fear factor." There is nothing more frightening than being in the ring with some big, ugly brute who is swinging at your head with everything he's got, if you have not prepared for the fight by giving 100 percent to your training and preparation. Because of the fear factor, I get up earlier, run further, train harder, and prepare mentally to the utmost for everything I do in the ring. Even a sparring session can be a very unpleasant experience if you haven't prepared properly. Because of this fear factor, I have always trained rigorously, won many more fights than I have lost, and have enjoyed the sport at a high level for many years. This has contributed to making me a better athlete, and helped me focus and perform at my best.

In fact, during my childhood and early adult years, I never really thought of myself as an athlete. Through boxing, I feel in middle age I have become one. By this I do not mean that I have any illusion that I could compete on a professional level in boxing or any other sport—far from it. I simply mean that I do many things that athletes do and I behave like an athlete in many ways—I train rigorously on a consistent basis, watch my diet at all times, limit severely any bad habits like smoking or drinking, and compete with others in the sport. I have been competing for more than 12 years, and have almost 20 white collar sparring matches under my belt. I intend to keep competing, because I love it, and I think it is good for me in many ways.

Because of these characteristics, I am convinced that boxing has helped me become a far better athlete than I would ever have been in any other sport. It has also helped me in innumerable ways to become a stronger human being and more successful businessman. It has strengthened my constitution and helped me to focus better on my work. It has sharpened my time-management skills, allowing me to set and achieve my goals in both athletics and business.

White collar boxing has added a dimension to my life that I am sure I would not have achieved in any other sport. Because it is so different, people respect that I do it, that I excel at it. In many ways, I have become "branded" as a boxer by many of my colleagues, clients, and other professionals with whom I work. The first thing many other businesspeople say to me when they see me is, "How's your boxing?" This is not all bad. Whether or not someone likes the sport of boxing or not, almost everyone would agree that the sport takes a great deal of focus, preparation, determination, and commitment. And what client would not want to do business with someone who demonstrates these four characteristics on a regular basis? What a person does in his personal life, or athletic life, spills over to his business life. In my opinion, it has netted me a huge plus.

All this being said, I still take careful measure to whom, and under what circumstances, I mention that I am a boxer. Some of my clients absolutely love it. Others seem offended by it. Certainly I have had instances in which clients or colleagues express a distaste for the sport when they hear that I practice it and I want to make sure that a discussion of boxing does not turn someone off. This, like anything else in business, is a judgment call, and there is no set formula for when and how it should be brought up in a discussion or business meeting. Once you do uncover someone who "gets" boxing, the bonding from that point on is complete. I am reminded of my first meeting with Senator Joe Bruno, the New York State Senate majority leader. Our meeting had been scheduled for 30 minutes of political discussion. We ended up spending two hours together discussing boxing, while his senior staff members stood by listening in amazement. At the end of the meeting, the senator and I had established a strong bond which has grown ever since.

In short, I view myself as a "regular guy," a businessman who tries to find the balance between making a living, staying in decent shape, and having time for a social life and family. I have chosen boxing as one way to accomplish this. I try to find a balance in my life on many levels. I have many interests and passions, and try to make room in my life for all of them. For that reason, time has become my biggest enemy. If someone is actively pursuing a career, it can be very hard to have the time to devote to a demanding workout schedule. This is true not only for someone who pursues boxing, but other sports and personal activities.

A professional boxer training for a fight trains hard two to three hours a day, plus road work and weights. Combine this with the mental preparation, study, and relaxation required, and it is a full-time job. The anxiety experienced by a white collar boxer can be just as great as that experienced by a professional boxer, the danger just as real. So how does a white collar boxer find the balance?

What lies beyond is the story of the evolution of white collar boxing or white collar sparring, its status in today's busy world, and the importance it has for those of us who love it. Most importantly, it is a story of the average person, the businessman or woman, the office worker, the family man, the recent college graduate, the policeman, the middle-aged overweight person, who has chosen boxing as a form of exercise and recreation. It is my story, but also the story of so many people I know, and hopefully many more who will experience this terrific sport in the future. It is truly the story of finding the balance in life, of paying attention to the things that can make a difference in how you look and feel, of how you treat others you know and care for, of being the best you can be. It is the story of one man's journey on this sometimes lonely road, which has taken him all over the world, and given him a recognition and respect that he would not have otherwise achieved. It is the story of how the sweet science profoundly affected my life.

And although I have not met Lennox Lewis, I can relate to him, and other professional and amateur boxers, in a very real way. However, to understand the importance of white collar boxing in today's world, I think it is important to understand the historical framework of the sport of boxing, of which white collar boxing is now an integral part.

CHAPTER 2

THE SWEET SCIENCE

Sweet Science of Bruising!
—PIERCE EGAN, *BOXIANA,* 1824

As a white collar boxer, I am proud to claim a small place in the history of mankind's oldest sport. To understand the contradictions in boxing, its brutishness and its grace, it helps to know how boxing has evolved.

Boxing has the greatest history of all sports, bar none. It dates back to 4000 B.C., if you believe the hieroglyphics of the ancient Egyptians. Ancient Sumerians, who lived in what is now Iraq, boxed at least five thousand years ago. Boxing is documented in ancient Greece as early as 1100 B.C. According to the writings of Elliott J. Gorn in *The Manly Art,* "A dangerous, bloody sport, boxing was considered good preparation for warfare, so men of great science and finesse received special praise. Boxers became exalted heroes, gladiators who celebrated the gods with their deeds and embodied the goal of unified mental, physical, and spiritual cultivation. Sports in general, and boxing in particular, were encouraged because they taught discipline while exemplifying Greek ideals of grace and beauty."

It was at the 23rd Olympiad of the Ancient Games in 688 B.C. when boxing first appeared on the program. It was something of a free-for-all, compared with today's sport. Though boxers were not allowed to bite each other, or to hit each other in the genital area, almost anything else was allowed, including kicking, gouging of eyes, pulling of hair, wrestling, and strangling. There were no rounds or weight classes. Boxers fought until one gave up, and raised a hand or finger in defeat. Boxers' tactics included shifting their positions to put the sun in their opponent's eyes, hitting with both hands, and using their thumbs to gouge the eyes of their adversary. The Greeks thought boxing the most demanding and dangerous of events, evidenced by ancient drawings that highlight scarred faces, bloody noses, and swollen ears. Deaths were recorded as the centuries evolved. It was not required that boxers wear clothes in the ancient games, and frequently they did not. "At the 23rd Olympiad, Onomastos (of Sicyon) became boxing's first gold-medalist, fighting nude, body gleaming with oil."

Boxing is recorded throughout the history of the Roman Empire. Developed as a spectator sport in ancient Rome, it was a favorite of Augustus, the first Roman emperor. Roman boxers wore leaded leather straps, which were later studded with iron spikes. The sport reached some of its bloodiest and most brutal moments in this era, although it was later overshadowed by gladiatorial combat. When the Roman Empire fell, so did boxing.

Although there are isolated references to boxing through the Middle Ages, it is not until the latter part of the seventeenth century in England, under the reign of Charles II, that boxing reemerges in any meaningful or recorded way. In 1681 a match between a footman and a butcher is cited in the annals of that era. In the early 1700s, James Figg, a wrestler and one of the most famous athletes in England's history, is given credit for introducing modern boxing to the world. Figg, who shaved his head to avoid hair-pulling, was an illiterate roustabout who was handy at defending himself both with a sword and his fists. Although others certainly had boxed before him, in 1719, at the age of 24 and as the result of his teaching and his exhibitions of skill, he became known as the Father of Boxing. He opened a boxing school in London, teaching his students a style of pugilism that would become known as bare-knuckle fighting. It is with Figg that the art and science of modern boxing begins.

The success of boxers has always been associated with their size. In the early years of English pugilism, however, there was only one "Champion," who most always tended to be what we would today call a "heavyweight." It was not until the late nineteenth century that the different weight classes were introduced, so that smaller men could have a fairer chance of winning a title. Even then, there were no universally recognized definitions of weight class.

Between 1812 and 1829, Pierce Egan published the five volumes of *Boxiana*, the first great writings of boxing history in which he chronicled the stories of many of the great English boxers of the eighteen and early nineteenth centuries. Egan referred to boxing as the "sweet science of bruising." This term floated out to the sport's followers with a poetic grace, with the intention of lending credibility and charm to the sport in the face of its critics. Throughout *Boxiana*, Egan constantly refers to boxing as science, or as scientific, hearkening to the fact that it required study and discipline. By describing boxing in this way, he lent a beauty and artistry to the sport. He saw science, strategy, and skill, where most observers saw chaos, brutality, and mayhem.

Intrigued by this concept, I spent some time pondering the meaning of the phrase. The word "sweet" has many confectionary and feminine connotations, but in this context it means "winning and persuasive." The word "science" is defined as "knowledge and skill." Putting the two words together has a truly artful meaning: "a winning and persuasive knowledge or skill that is accumulated and established over time."

However, one wonders how the terms "sweet" and "science" could have been applied to the sport in Egan's time. There was no governing body to legitimize it. Reminiscent of the ancient Greek and Roman eras, there were no rest periods, and fights lasted until one of the boxers could no longer continue. Fights had the haphazard and unrefined aura of street fights, with some fighters resorting to gouging, biting, and kicking, instead of throwing punches. *Sweet science* indeed! When the term was coined, the sport was seemingly neither sweet nor scientific.

Egan saw an ethereal presence to the sport: "Boxing has always had an appeal to imaginative minds; the elemental nature of the conflict, the uncertain drama of the fight, the variety of character in those who submit themselves to the ordeal; perhaps these explain part of the attraction." Egan also argued that boxing taught lessons in humanity and civility, settling aggravated disputes with the same final measure as could be realized by using knives or pistols, but without the accompanying loss of life or permanent injury.

One famous English boxer whom Egan discusses in great detail is Jack Broughton, universally recognized as the "Father of the English School of Boxing." Broughton was six feet tall, weighed almost 200 pounds, and, like Figg, had shaved his head. Using his intelligence and cunning to overcome opponents in the ring, he fought with style and introduced defensive measures such as ring movement and blocking, often hitting and then retreating.

Broughton took the sport one step further towards the modern era in 1743 when he introduced rules, which eventually became the standard for most boxing matches of that era. Broughton's rules were the first standards imposed on this very unregulated and unsupervised sport. These guidelines prohibited hitting below the belt and the striking of a fallen opponent. A round ended when a man hit the ground, and a

thirty-second rest period was taken. Following that, both boxers were required to toe a mark called the "scratch" in the
middle of the ring. Each boxer could now appoint seconds, or
corner men, to assist them between rounds. Boxing referees
(called "umpires"), whose decisions were final, were also introduced. These changes brought a more refined tone to the ring,
and guided prize fighting for almost 100 years, from 1743
through 1838.

As boxing became more well known, it attracted more spectators from the aristocracy and upper classes. Even royalty,
including the Prince of Wales and the Duke of York, showed up
at ringside on occasion during this era. Boxing was very popular, and the "fancy," as the spectators were called, came to follow
the sport with great interest, as the "bulldog courage" displayed
in the ring stirred in them both a sense of national pride and
masculinity. At the same time, boxing crossed over many social
and economic barriers, allowing the upper classes to cement
ties with social and class inferiors in their common link to the
sport, while giving them the platform to display evidence of
wealth, status, and power.

Broughton, who should be credited with some of the earli-
est marketing advances of the sport, also conducted boxing
classes at the Haymarket Academy in London, where they were
advertised as "instructions in the mystery of boxing, the wholly
British art for gentlemen." As Egan describes it, Broughton
"drew crowds after him to witness his exhibitions; there was
neatness about his method completely new, and unknown to his
auditors (audience), he stopped the blows aimed at any part of
him by his antagonists with so much skill, and hit his many
ways with so much ease, that he astonished and terrified his
opponents beyond measure." Like all great masters of an art
or craft, Broughton generally exhibited something new in
every contest. He did not depend upon any particular blow or
maneuver. "The eye of Broughton was most lively and acute,
so perceiving the weakness of any adversary; and, his arm

keeping pace with that valuable assistant, protected him from the most destructive blows; and his quick penetration made him always aware of any direct intent pursued by his adversary, as immediately to render it futile and unavailing. His guard was considered so complete, that his frame appeared as well secured as if in a fence; uncommon strength and bottom (courage) often fell before him. His various attitudes in the fight were fine and impressive, and his countenance always animated and cheerful." Broughton became the athletic star of his day; his talents as a boxer gained him many admirers and patrons. He was an amiable man, very smart, and communicated well. His involvement in boxing was very positive for the sport.

Egan may have been clairvoyant in his writing. Twentieth-century fighters such as Muhammad Ali and Sugar Ray Robinson would cause the world to revisit the term sweet science for its true embodiment. In Egan's own time, however, few fighters exuded that kind of style and grace in the ring. It would be decades and into another century before the readers of *Boxiana* would see fighters exploit scientific training regimens, such as aerobics and weight training, and combine them with diet and nutrition.

In the late eighteenth century, Daniel Mendoza, a boxer of Spanish-English descent became the first prominent Jewish boxer and the 16th Champion of England. The development of boxing as a really scientific proposition reached a heightened level in the able and quick hands of this extraordinary young boxer, who reigned as champion from 1791 to 1795. Only five feet, seven inches in height, and weighing approximately 160 pounds, this small man was able to overcome much larger adversaries with the use of skill and agility. Many boxing critics of his day wrote enthusiastically about his ring generalship and superb science. "Others, though these were in the minority, complained that there was something cowardly about a fighter who frequently retreated and relied on superior agility and speed to win rather than standing up in true British bulldog style and hammering away doggedly until he or his opponent dropped. Thus he revolutionized the Prize Ring. His advent ended the reign of the crude slugger." Despite the efforts of Broughton and Mendoza, however, for most of the eighteenth and nineteenth centuries, the sweet science was yet to emerge in its truest form.

Most boxers of the day were more skilled at rough-and-tumble fighting. James "Deaf" Burke, for instance, the 29th Champion of England, fought Simon Byrne of Ireland in 1833 in the longest championship fight on record, lasting ninety-nine rounds over a time span of three hours and sixteen minutes. Burke won, and unfortunately Byrne died of his injuries sustained during the epic battle. Burke later drifted to America to fight after he felt ill-treated by critics following the death of his opponent, Simon Byrne. Eventually, Burke faced another Irishman, Sam O'Rourke, who was determined to avenge Byrne's death. O'Rourke was a gambler and gangster, and slandered Burke at every opportunity. They fought in New Orleans in 1836, but the fight ended when O'Rourke's mobster friends cut the ropes and attacked Burke, who was winning the fight. Burke fled back to New York for one more fight and then returned to England. He lost his title in 1839 to William Abednego Thompson, known as "Bold Bendingo," a southpaw who won the championship from Burke on a foul.

In 1872, John Sholto Douglas, a British sportsman also known as the Marquess of Queensberry, sponsored a new boxing code that was to bear his name. The "Marquess of Queensberry Rules," as they eventually became known, were amazingly simple and revolutionized the sport. A 24-foot square ring was to be used. Boxers were required to wear gloves, given a ten-second count after a knockdown, allowed to fight for three-minute rounds, and given one-minute rest periods between rounds. However, these rules were slow to be enacted, and were not uniformly followed in all fight venues of the nineteenth century.

By the early part of the nineteenth century, boxing had reached America, where it was born of slavery. Boxing was a source of amusement for Southern plantation owners who put together their strongest and most able-bodied slaves to fight each other for gambling and sport. The enslaved combatants often wore iron collars and fought to the point of death. The cruelty of these matches drew the attention of Frederick Douglass, who protested the practice.

By the mid-nineteenth century, there were three principal competitive sports in the United States—track and field, swimming, and boxing. By the early 1860s, prize fighting had reached a high water mark, as the Civil War helped familiarize countless men with pugilism. Sparring matches were part of regular camp entertainments. In some cases, boxing was used as a means to resolve conflicts between soldiers. There was a perceived connection between boxing and warfare. Both had an element of violence at their core, and demanded a great deal of courage and sacrifice. Both inhabited a world of physical conflict, and required discipline and strategy to overcome the odds against them.

Sports in general gained greater acceptance towards the turn of the century; they were viewed as a necessary counterbalance to the somewhat complacent life Americans enjoyed during that era of prosperity. As people began to realize the benefits of science and technology, doctors gained stature and confidence in the public eye. Their advice to overweight and stressed-out Americans was to improve their personal habits and exercise. John Boyle O'Reilly, a poet and editor of the *Boston Pilot*, became a vocal and articulate advocate, writing that "sparring was the perfect recreation for businessmen whose nerves were frayed by competition and energies depleted by the frenetic pace of life. No other sport exercised the trunk, limbs, eyes, and mind so well. The intensity of sparring made it ideal training for the young: The boxer in action has not a loose muscle or a sleepy brain cell. His mind is quicker and more watchful than a chess player's. He has to gather his impulses and hurl them, straight and purposeful, with every moment and motion." Could these nineteenth-century passages be the first historical reference to the future emergence of white collar boxing?

As the century wore on, boxing became a social register sport—the Astors, the Vanderbilts, the Roosevelts and other prominent families could be found sparring in gyms in New York City. A sickly child, young Theodore Roosevelt began boxing at Harvard College to build up his health and keep fellow students from teasing him. It was not long until he earned respect from his classmates who had earlier ridiculed him. Boxing became his hobby, and he became a voracious advocate of the sport. He even felt it should be a part of the public school system. Roosevelt sparred whenever he got a chance, even in the White House, where he was also visited by John L. Sullivan, the last bare-knuckle champion.

In that era, the "Great John L." Sullivan epitomized American boxing. He emerged on February 2, 1882, when at the age of 23, he laid out Paddy Ryan, the heavyweight champion of the world, in a mere three rounds to become the new champion. Sullivan, also known as the "Boston Strong Boy," was idolized by millions as a true working-class hero, who trained by walking mile after mile through the working class neighborhoods of Boston, stopping at every saloon along the way to proclaim he could "lick any son-of-a-bitch in the house." As America's champion, his legend as a roaring, hard-drinking, even harder-hitting, man of the world spread far and wide. While champion, he issued an offer to pay $1,000 to any man who could stand four three-minute rounds with him, and toured the United States to find people who would accept the challenge. Along the way, he knocked out dozens of opponents, and became firmly established at the pinnacle of public fame. The first superstar in the American sports landscape, he was well-known throughout the entire country for his ability to out-box and out-drink anyone who stood in his way.

Actually, big John L. was not that big in stature, certainly not by today's heavyweight division standards. He stood 5'11" and weighed 180 pounds, a light heavyweight in today's weight categories. But his Irish-American, working class background helped him become a symbol of the raw spirit of the country, which was big and tough and sprawling. Though he enjoyed the good life that his success had brought him, he never forgot his working-class origins. It became known that he had a softness in his heart for people less fortunate than he, and he was constantly reaching into his pocket for a five-, ten-, or twenty-dollar bill to give to a down-and-out person, as he would meet them on the street. Possibly the nation's most famous citizen at the time, John L. Sullivan reigned as champion for ten years from 1882 until 1892, and fought in the last bare-knuckle championship fight in July 1889, when he defeated Jake Kilrain in the 75th round under a blazing sun in Richburg, Mississippi.

In 1892, Sullivan agreed to a fight with "Gentleman Jim" Corbett, the first American championship fight to be held under the Marquess of Queensberry rules. The date for the first heavyweight championship bout fought with gloves was set for September 7, 1892, in New Orleans. The front pages of newspapers across the country saw the presidential campaign of Benjamin Harrison and Grover Cleveland take a back seat, as the country enthusiastically watched the drama of the fight unfurl as the date drew near. Unfortunately, Sullivan had not done any serious fighting since his match with Jake Kilrain three years earlier, and on the night of the fight, his flabby body bore evidence of that. To the surprise of many, the fight was really no contest. Sullivan seemed lost, a barroom brawler matched against a pugilistic artist. Corbett, as elegant as Sullivan was brutish, jabbed, danced, and circled Sullivan, until finally Corbett scored a knockout over Sullivan in the 21st round. Corbett was a forerunner to boxers of the modern era—he trained heavily, strategized to win fights, and fought wearing gloves.

In the twentieth century, boxing enjoyed some of its greatest moments of glory. There was probably no one more flashy or controversial than Jack Johnson, a black man who threatened the conventional wisdom of the day, which was ensconced in racial bigotry, by driving fast cars, sipping vintage wines through a straw, dating and marrying white women, and convincingly beating any boxer who got in his way. Possibly the most reviled black man of his time, he openly flaunted his sexuality in front of reporters who watched him train, at times wrapping his penis in gauze and displaying its magnificence by wearing tight shorts. He became the first African-American heavyweight champion on Boxing Day, December 26, 1908, when he defeated Tommy Burns in 14 rounds in Sydney, Australia.

Johnson, who stood 6'1¼" and weighed approximately 210 pounds, was a master of ring science. Sporting an intimidating stance, his great defensive skills made him an elusive target. His punishing stiff jabs, combined with his ring agility, feinting ability and fluid movement, made him the most feared boxer of his time. His personal activities outside the ring kept him in sharp focus of the critical public eye. Jim Jeffries, who had retired as heavyweight champion in 1904, was called off his farm by the demanding and vengeful public to fight Johnson on July 4, 1910, in Reno, Nevada, and was soundly defeated by Johnson.

A worldwide search then ensued for a "White Hope" to beat Johnson, and bring the title back to a Caucasian heavyweight. Although there were many would-be contenders for this prize, none seemed worthy until 6'6" Jess Willard appeared, and earned public respect by besting several good heavyweights and gaining national recognition. The fight between Willard and Johnson took place on April 5, 1915, on the outskirts of Havana, Cuba, in the broiling sun. Johnson, then 37 years old, was knocked out by Willard in the 26th round, although Johnson was ahead on the cards at the time.

In the Roaring Twenties, Jack Dempsey captured the imagination of a country that still treasured toughness and individuality. A charismatic individual with fierce good looks and a lineage that was part Cherokee Indian, Dempsey embodied an era whose time frame ran roughly from 1919, when Prohibition began, until 1929, when the stock market crashed. Dempsey, whose handle was "the Manassa Mauler," was a bruiser, the John L. Sullivan of his time (minus some of the bad habits), who would accept five punches for the privilege of delivering one. He played a leading man's role in a number of boxing "firsts," including the quickest knockout in a heavyweight bout of national importance, when he defeated Carl Morris in fourteen seconds in New Orleans on December 16, 1918, and the first million dollar gate against Georges Carpentier on July 2, 1921. It seemed that every time Jack Dempsey defended his title, an epic battle ensued. His sensational battle on September 14, 1923 against Luis Angel Firpo, the "Wild Bull of the Pampas," in which Dempsey was knocked out of the ring before going on to win by knockout, was immortalized by the artist George Bellows in his classic and timeless work *Dempsey versus Firpo.*

The match-ups in 1926 and 1927 between Jack Dempsey and Gene Tunney were a classic of a brawler versus a boxer, and resulted in one of the most controversial battles in boxing history, the famous "Battle of the Long Count." In the second of their two highly charged contests on September 22, 1927, Dempsey knocked down the highly skilled Tunney in the seventh round but lost precious seconds by failing to go to a neutral corner before the count began. Tunney rose to his feet at the count of nine, after the count had been delayed by several seconds, then went on to win the fight by decision. As evidence of the commercial popularity of the sport at this time, this fight at Soldier's Field in Chicago marked the first $2 million gate in history, a huge sum of money in that era.

Gene Tunney was a delicate man in a savage sport, tall and handsome. He had been a Marine in World War I and had learned his boxing skills as a member of the American Expeditionary Force, where he became light heavyweight champion in France. Tunney was gentle and articulate outside the ring, an avid reader, and remarkably composed and artistic inside the ring—a perfect ambassador for the sweet science. One of the most clinically clever heavyweight boxers ever, in later years, he would lecture at Yale. Inside the ring, he was elusive as a "wisp of smoke." By the time Dempsey and Tunney dueled in their two legendary encounters, Dempsey had achieved legendary status. Tunney won both fights, but it is Dempsey who history remembers more favorably, as his image of a rogue and savage ring general were backed up with fists of steel and an iron jaw. As an indication of the power and public interest that the sport of boxing commanded in this era, the day after the first battle between the two, the story covered the front page of the *New York Times*, including a three tier banner headline, accompanied by seven pages of coverage in the front section.

The fights between Max Schmeling and Joe Louis in 1936 and 1938 were symbolic of the clashing of two nations, Germany and the United States, as the world reacted to the buildup of the German war machine in anticipation of World War II. It all started in 1936, when the Berlin Olympics had been used by the Nazi propaganda machine as a forum to promote Aryan superiority. In truth, Schmeling was a decent man in conflict with the Nazi regime and racial policies of Hitler's Third Reich. Hitler had asked Schmeling to join the Nazi Party on several occasions, and Schmeling had declined to do so. However, in the eyes of many people in America, Schmeling became a symbol of Nazi Germany. The honor of the two strongest countries in the world was at stake when Max

Schmeling and Joe Louis finally met in 1936. The eyes of the world turned to Yankee Stadium in New York, where the fights occurred. Many were shocked when, in the 12th round of their epic fight, Schmeling knocked out the previously undefeated Louis in their first grueling match on June 19, 1936.

Louis was to avenge this loss on June 22, 1938, with a dramatic first-round knockout that left no doubt about his superiority over Schmeling. Among those who followed the fights with keen interest was Adolf Hitler, whose steadfast belief in the superiority of the Aryan race was severely challenged on the world stage by the results of the second fight. He never forgave Schmeling and had him sent on suicide missions as a paratrooper during the war. Schmeling's injuries in this fight had landed him in the hospital, where Louis visited him. Though separated by the war, geography, and the struggles of the era, Schmeling and Louis were to reconnect in later years, and maintained a mutual respect and friendship for each other. Louis, who later fell on hard times through mismanagement of his personal finances, was quietly aided financially in later years by Schmeling, who had used his prize winnings in boxing to purchase the Coca-Cola franchise in Germany and grew wealthy in the postwar era. Schmeling also paid for Louis's funeral in 1981.

As the mid-twentieth century dawned, new and exciting boxers began to appear. Some took the sport to new levels of ring artistry and skill. In his book *Inside Boxing*, Robert Seltzer captured this movement in the sport when he stated, "Hell is not roped off. The ring is. And that may be the only difference between the two venues. Boxing is a ballistic ballet, a sport that can be lovely one minute, ugly the next. The beauty? Well, it is embodied in wondrous athletes such as Sugar Ray Robinson and Muhammad Ali, both of whom turned the ring into a ballroom, their movements so precise they appeared to be choreographed. But the beauty is everywhere . . . a dip of the shoulder here, a twitch of the head there. Poetry in motion?"

Perhaps no one more epitomized the term sweet science than Sugar Ray Robinson. In 1997, *Ring Magazine* bestowed upon him a title as the greatest fighter who ever lived. Robinson was known to throw the best combinations in boxing history. He had an amazing arsenal of punches, and could throw combinations with blinding speed from almost any angle—firing uppercuts off hooks and hooks off right hands. His offensive moves were so powerful that his superb defense was often unnecessary, as many of his opponents failed to retaliate from a barrage of punches to the body and head. Muhammad Ali believed him to be the greatest fighter of all time, and fashioned much of his ring movement after him. He was impressed that Robinson could dance and throw punches while backing up. Said Eddie Futch, a great trainer who worked with more than 15 world champions, "There were great fighters before Robinson, but it was Robinson who put everything together in one package—speed, grace, and power. . . . Sugar Ray Robinson represented the finest qualities you can find in a boxer—his style, his class, his grace and his consummate artistry. He could box, and he could punch. You wouldn't expect a ballet dancer to be able to kill you with one punch, but Robinson could."

Sugar Ray Robinson compiled a professional record of 175-19-6, including 110 knockouts. (The first number indicates wins; the second, losses; the third, draws.) Of his losses, 18 came after the age of 30. Prior to that he had only been defeated by Jake LaMotta, "The Raging Bull," whose life was dramatized in a movie by the same name starring Robert DeNiro. On February 5, 1943, LaMotta won against Robinson by decision. Robinson avenged this loss by victories on five other occasions. LaMotta, like Rocky Marciano in later years, had no fear. A fighter with no fear has a sense of confidence, which manifests itself in a carelessness and courageousness that makes him very dangerous. Though he lacked the physical attributes of Sugar Ray

Robinson, this lack of fear made Jake LaMotta a formidable opponent for Robinson.

On February 14, 1951, LaMotta, clearly beaten by Robinson in the thirteenth round, exhausted and hanging on the ropes, refused to be knocked down by Robinson despite the tremendous barrage of punches Robinson threw at him. This, the last of their six encounters, which spanned almost a decade, is considered one of the greatest fights of all time. LaMotta won the crowd that night with his guts and sheer will and determination, even though Robinson won the fight and LaMotta's middleweight crown. As Robinson celebrated his well-deserved victory, LaMotta was elevated to boxing immortality.

Five years after this dramatic fight, *New Yorker* writer A.J. Liebling published an updated version of Pierce Egan's boxing history. *The Sweet Science* is considered one of the greatest sports books ever written, and features bouts from the 1920s through the 1950s. For my money, the original *Boxiana* more appropriately conveys the meaning of the sweet science, but Liebling's *The Sweet Science* is an excellent overview of that era of boxing; Liebling makes constant comparisons between the boxing of his day and that of Pierce Egan.

The great undefeated heavyweight champion, Rocky Marciano, is one of the legends described in *The Sweet Science*. In an insightful passage, Liebling quotes noted psychiatrist Dr. J.L. Moreno, who observed Marciano before his second championship fight with Ezzard Charles in September of 1954. "Marciano has presence of mind," Dr. Moreno wrote. "That is the most important thing—a most decisive factor in the ring. Absence of mind is most devastating to a pugilist. Marciano has the ability to concentrate immediately on the crisis. . . . He is not calculable. His concentration is intense…Marciano has no inhibitions. . . . Rocky is positive and supremely confident. He has no fears to hold him back. He is of one piece."

Although Rocky Marciano can hardly be described as the free-form, artistic, ballet-dancer type that might characterize the likes of Jim Corbett, Gene Tunney, Sugar Ray Robinson, Muhammad Ali, and others, this mindfulness of purpose and application of technique helps explain Marciano's remarkable string of 49 victories and no defeats in his professional boxing career. Before the second bout with Charles, Dr. Moreno wrote about Marciano, "He has poise, charm, sensitivity, imagination, a remarkable retentive memory, and a rugged handsomeness." To be frank, this is not the image I have retained of Rocky Marciano. What I recall from the images I have of him on radio and television as I was growing up, is that he seemed impervious to pain—perhaps this is the most telling characteristic of his abilities, and one of his secrets in his mastery of the sweet science. Of one thing there is no doubt: Rocky Marciano was his own man.

This impression was confirmed when I studied old fight tapes of Rocky Marciano. The study of old tapes and fight videos is something people who love the sport do all the time. I have a library of old tapes of both professional and white collar fights, including a tape of every fight I was in. When I hear that I am going to fight an experienced fighter, the first thing I do is try to find a tape on him. By studying these tapes, I might be able to spot a technical flaw and exploit it. If I'm not mistaken, studying Joe Louis's tapes helped Max Schmeling defeat him the first time.

In my lifetime, it is Muhammad Ali who best demonstrates the sweet science. Described as a "force of nature," Ali gave boxing a new look of grace and smoothness through his disciplined training, incredibly fast hands and footwork, and his ability to glide effortlessly through a fight. The fight on March 8, 1971, between Muhammad Ali and Joe Frazier at Madison Square Garden in New York was much more than a boxing match. Agitated by the lingering wounds of the Vietnam conflict, it was symbolic of the radical side of our country, as represented by Ali, confronting the more traditional side of our country, as represented by Frazier. The entire country stopped to watch and listen to this fight. I was in Milwaukee, Wisconsin at the time of this fight, and paid $25 to see it at a local movie theater, which was packed to the gills. The crowd was on its feet (at a movie theater!) for much of the fight. Although there was much ebb and flow in this epic struggle between the two combatants, I remember feeling helpless as Frazier knocked down Ali, who I was pulling for, in the fifteenth round. Ali was out on his feet as the fight ended, and moments later, Frazier's hand was raised to acknowledge his victory by decision. Despite his loss to Frazier that night, Ali could never be denied his indelible position in boxing history.

Through the great fighters, from "Gentleman Jim" Corbett to Gene Tunney to Sugar Ray Robinson to Muhammad Ali, boxing developed into a sport of skill and cunning that epitomizes the sweet science. Boxers such as Sugar Ray Leonard, Roy Jones, Jr., and Oscar De La Hoya have performed with such ease and grace that they could just as easily have mastered ballet or ballroom dancing. Through them, the sweet science has come of age in our lifetimes.

This grand history of a great sport laid the foundation from which white collar boxing was born. I find it interesting that nothing quite like white collar boxing developed over the ages—there was never a bridge from the professional ranks to the average citizen until the latter part of the twentieth century. Perhaps it seemed to most people that the lofty boundaries of the sweet science were simply out of reach. Fortunately for me and thousands white collar boxers today, this did not prove to be correct.

CHAPTER

3

FROM PECOS, TEXAS, TO NEW YORK CITY

George and I grew up in West Texas where the sky seems endless and so do the possibilities.
—FIRST LADY LAURA BUSH

It is fun for me to look back on my career as a white collar boxer, and reflect on the many steps I took along the way. In many ways, it was unlikely that I would become a successful white collar boxer. There were many obstacles, diversions, and reasons to simply not do it. However, there are reasons why I gravitated to boxing. In one sense, I had been around boxing all my life. It certainly had found its way to Pecos, Texas, my home town.

As a little boy, I remember sitting in our kitchen after supper, watching my dad putter in his workshop behind our house. He was always using his hands to build and fix things. I never saw him work on anything that he could not fix. He was good at all kinds of handiwork, such as carpentry, plumbing, and metalwork. Every night he would tinker for a couple of hours, before going to bed. This was how he relaxed.

My father was a classic Texan, born in 1893, the son of a cowboy. He was a cowboy himself for the first 30 years of his life. His name was Irbin Gary Oden, but everyone called him I.G. He was born on a ranch, and worked as a ranch hand for the early part of his life. He did two tours in the army with the U.S. Calvary, back when they used to ride horses. He had completed one tour of duty, but World War I broke out and he volunteered for another. At one point, he was guarding the Texas and Arizona borders along the Rio Grande against Pancho Villa, the Mexican outlaw. After returning to civilian life and working as a cowboy for many years, he eventually moved into the small town of Pecos, Texas, where his father, my grandfather Bill Arp Oden, also a former cowboy, had settled.

My father was a tall, lean man, very rugged looking, the type you used to see in Marlboro cigarette commercials. He smoked "Bull Durham" for all of his life, which was a tobacco that had to be rolled by hand into cigarettes. He always wore khakis and a big hat. As my mother, Violet Evans Oden, used to say, "He was a man of few words, but you listened to every one of them." His voice had a way of cutting right through you. You did not talk back to my dad.

What I remember most about my dad, as I watched him in his workshop after dinner, was the size and shape of his arms. He wore his khaki shirt during the day. On warm evenings, he would remove it and wear only a ribbed, sleeveless undershirt. He had extraordinary arms. He was a thin man, yet his arms had the largest bulging muscles I had ever seen, all cables and cords, surrounded by big manly veins that ran up and down beneath his skin. When he would pick up a pencil or a hammer, his muscle would double the size of the arm. I would sit in amazement.

Pecos was the home of the world's first rodeo, dating back to 1883. It was a small cotton farming town, and a pretty good place to grow up. There wasn't a lot to do but play sports and go to church. My father was a huge boxing fan. He subscribed to one magazine—*Ring* magazine. We did not have a television set when I was a small boy, but we had a radio. On Friday nights, there was a boxing program on the radio, and Dad and I would listen to it every week. There were always at least a couple of fights. I have a faint memory of the radio broadcast of the Rocky Marciano–Archie Moore fight on September 21, 1955, when Archie Moore collapsed in his own corner in the ninth round of a furious battle in which Marciano was knocked down early in the bout. Later, after my family acquired a television, Dad and I watched Ingemar Johansson of Sweden send Floyd Patterson to the floor seven times in the third round on the way to his June 26, 1959 victory. We watched Patterson avenge this loss to Johansson by a fifth round knockout on June 22, 1960. I grew to love the sport at an early age, and it was a great way for my father and me to spend time together.

As a little boy, my dad bought me two pairs of boxing gloves. When my friends would come over to play with me, my dad would bring out the gloves and have us box. I was always a little bigger than most of my friends, and can never remember losing a match. However, it seemed that rarely would my friends come over to see me when they knew my father was going to be there. I suppose that this was because they knew my father would put the gloves on us, and they thought I was a better boxer than they were! This gave me some confidence in my boxing at a very young age.

My grandfather died when I was five years old, and shortly thereafter my grandmother died. My parents inherited their house, which they made into a rental house. The house was set up in such a way that three different parts of it could be rented out. This was during the 1950s in West Texas, and times were not the best. My father would frequently have to go over to this house to collect the rent when it was due. I remember that one apartment unit was rented to a very tall, burly young man, who had a very attractive wife. They had come to our home when they first rented the house. He was a big friendly guy, a truck driver. Apparently, he was laid off after a few months, and could not produce the rent for some period of time. My father was a very fair man, and worked with this guy for months, hoping he would eventually get back on his feet. I could see his patience was wearing thin. My dad drove a pickup truck—he worked as a superintendent at the city water department. One evening he asked me if I wanted to go for a ride, which I always did. I climbed into the pickup truck and off we went. Dad and I went to the front door, and the big man answered. Dad was looking for the rent payment, which had been promised to him four weeks earlier. The man was very apologetic, but no rent check was produced. Dad apparently had had enough of this, and the man promised to have it to my dad the next night, without fail. My dad was not the kind of person you could promise something to and not deliver.

The next night we went back to the rental house, and were greeted by the big man in the parking lot. He had a tale of woe, and no rent check. Dad reminded him of his promise, in no uncertain terms. The big man just shrugged his shoulders, and turned his back to walk away. My dad was about six feet tall, and at least 60 years old at the time. Despite his muscled frame, he was very thin; I doubt he weighed 170 pounds. The big man must have been at least 6'4", and in his mid-twenties. He must have weighed 220 pounds. In a flash, my father reached up and grabbed his shoulder, whirled him around, and hit him in the chest hard enough to send him to the ground. The big man just sat there in disbelief, and asked, "Why did you do that?" My father said, "Because you lied to me. Now tell me when I will get my money." The man said he would bring it to our home the next night, and that's exactly what he did. He lived in the rental house for another 18 months, and never missed another rent payment.

That experience really impressed me. First of all, that my father could actually be that tough. Secondly, that he had the courage to stand up to this younger, stronger, bigger man. And lastly, that the ability to use your fists could really come in handy in certain situations.

As a boy growing up in Pecos, Texas, I found plenty of opportunities to defend myself. It was a small, clean town, but had a real Western, cowboy flair—lots of jeans and cowboy boots in Pecos. There was a lot of farming and ranching in the area. Cowboys are tough guys, and there was always an undercurrent of someone ready and willing to square off in a fight with someone else about something.

It seemed I was always getting into fights. Nothing serious, that's just the way it was growing up in West Texas at that time. A schoolboy had to be ready to defend himself at any time. I believe that I won all of my fights in the early years rather easily because I was bigger, and because I had the experience of boxing in my backyard due to my dad's influence.

Then came Paul Greer. He was the new kid in school in the fourth grade at Pecos Elementary, and no one knew anything about him. One of my friends, Richard Hart, who was always a promoter/agitator, introduced me to Paul Greer one day on the playground. He said to me, "This is Paul Greer, and he's tough." These were fighting words to me. I said, "He's not as tough as I am." "Oh, yes he is," said Richard, "and he can prove it."

Well, a fight was promoted by Richard Hart for after school that day. It was held behind my music teacher's house, across the street from our school. Paul Greer showed up, and we went at it. Indeed, he was very tough, and he hit me with some good hard shots, which resulted in a black eye for me. The fight went on for some time, but I had a clear sense that it was not going my way. I was prepared to stick it out, though, until someone came running over to tell us that the principal of the school was coming. So I ran. No way was I going to get caught in the act of fighting. I wasn't running from Paul Greer, but as I looked back over my shoulder, Paul asked, "What are you running from, John?" Of course, the whole school told the story the next day that I was losing the fight with Paul Greer, and ran away. In my mind, that was not true—if the principal hadn't been coming, I would definitely not have left the fight scene. Right then I could tell that not everything people say about a boxing match is necessarily true—there's always room for interpretation. The experience caused me to be more cautious about my opponents, though, and not to just get into fights for the heck of it.

I played a lot of baseball in my early years—it took up a lot of my time until I was about 13. I was pretty good as a Little Leaguer. We had a great team, and almost made the state tournament, but were knocked out in the last game by a town smaller than us. I had won the batting trophy that year, and had the third best pitching record in the league. When I was not pitching, my regular position was first base. But the guy who was considered the big hitter was Curtiss Winterrowd. He hit the most home runs. He looked a little like Babe Ruth, same stocky build. He had a great batting stance, and was a true home run hitter. He batted in the coveted fourth position, the power spot, even though I was the best hitter overall—at least I had the best batting average. I batted fifth, which was a spot I always liked and at which I performed well. It was also a less threatening spot than fourth position, less pressure. Nevertheless, with a 0.426 batting average in the regular season, I was good for a hit almost one out of every two trips to the plate, and our team worked well together and we could usually win the big games.

Curtiss Winterrowd was also considered a tough guy, and always seemed ready to fight at the drop of a hat. He ran a good bluff, and I stayed out of his way. But he was one of those kids who razzed the other kids, and he razzed me as much as he did anyone. Perhaps it was because I won the batting trophy that year, I don't know. Anyway I was around him a lot, on road trips and practice sessions. Every now and then, he would taunt me in a way that could have easily led to a confrontation. However, I never returned his taunts or put myself in a position where there was no alternative but to fight. Maybe it was the experience I had with Paul Greer. But I certainly remember his badgering me on a number of occasions, and I did not appreciate it. I was waiting for the right time to get even.

One of my part-time jobs in Pecos was running the bowling alley on Sundays. I would work at the counter checking people in and out, taking money for bowling, fitting them with shoes, et cetera. It was a great job. I hung around the bowling alley a lot, and bowled all the time. I was also in a Saturday morning bowling league with Curtis Winterrowd. One Saturday when I was 13 or 14 (past the age of Little League), our team met at the bowling alley for our Saturday morning competition. I had made a decision that if Curtis Winterrowd said one cross word to me, I was going to let him have it. It was *my* time. Well, he didn't disappoint me. He started in on me, and I stood up and hit him full force with a stomach punch. He doubled over and went to the floor. That was it—fight over, bully put in his place. I never had any more problems with Curtis Winterrowd. Another lesson I learned from boxing at a young age—pick your opponents and times carefully, plan diligently, and execute your strategy quickly.

In high school, I was a very active student, with a lot of extracurricular activities, including sports. I also held several part-time jobs, and was very busy. I had my share of friends, and even began to date. I started to get taller, and developed the same lean frame as my father. I soon grew to over six feet, and continued growing throughout high school. As I got older, I never particularly excelled at athletics, but found I could do okay at almost any sport I tried. But on the other hand, I was not a natural "jock," and never felt that I was going to be the star of any team, like I had been back in my Little League days.

One evening I was out with a number of friends in connection with a social event at high school. For some reason, as

I was running across a front lawn, I tripped on a sidewalk. When I did this, I heard my foot pop, and knew something bad had happened. After driving around for a while, I was aware that my foot was in a great deal of pain. When I got home, I limped past my parents in our kitchen, continuing on back to my bedroom. I was apparently limping badly, and my mother asked me what had happened. "I think I broke my foot," was my reply. Mother said, "How did it happen?" I snapped at her, "I tripped, how do you *think* it happened?" Then I continued on back into my bedroom. I heard my father's footsteps behind me, saying, "John, come here." By the time I got to my bedroom, I heard him right behind me. I knew he wanted to hit me. Keep in mind, at this point he was almost 70 years old. I was 16 years old. I managed to duck out of his way, as he swung hard at me. I did not even think of swinging back—he was my dad! He was maneuvering toward me, a very angry look in his face, when I laid back on the bed. I said, "Dad, my foot is broken." He said, "Don't ever talk to your mother that way again." He stood glaring over me for about 30 seconds, ready to swing again if provoked, and left the room. I breathed a sign of relief. Another lesson—there are times and people you just don't want to fight, no matter what.

My father never talked about himself. He was born at the end of another era—the "Old West." He was born to be a ranch hand, a cowboy, a Cavalryman. He was the epitome of the strong, silent type. In many ways, when I knew him, he was out of his element. Time had passed him by. I never asked him how much he had fought in his younger days—he got those arms from somewhere. He never went to the gym or lifted weights. He did tell me one thing, "John, don't ever get in a fight. You're either going to kill someone or get yourself killed." I always wondered what was behind that axiom, from his past. In any case, my boxing has taught me that in the real world, it's not a bad philosophy.

As I went further in high school, I disconnected more and more with athletics. I never really connected with football or basketball and grew away from baseball after my Little League days. Also, my part-time jobs took a lot of my time after school. I liked making my own money so I would not have to ask my parents for spending money. I also loved giving my mother presents, as she never bought things for herself. Plus, I wanted to save so I could go to college.

I graduated from the University of Texas at Austin. I had moved on to graduate school there when I found myself facing the draft during the Vietnam War. I had no desire to go to Vietnam, and joined the Texas National Guard as a paratrooper in the infantry. During my service, I made eight parachute jumps. After the army, I took a summer vacation in Europe, where I went to most of the major countries and cities of Europe, and had a great time. On the way back to Austin to finish graduate school, I stopped in New York City, and spent two of the most incredible days and nights of my life. I took an all-day bus tour of the city, went to Broadway plays, hung out in Times Square, and walked up and down Fifth Avenue. Within 24 hours, I decided that New York was the greatest city in the world, and I knew it was going to be a big part of my future. After graduation from the University of Texas with an MBA, and a brief stint in Milwaukee, Wisconsin, I decided it was time for me to fulfill my destiny—I was on my way to New York City.

I landed a job at Bankers Trust Company, and began my career in financial services. Every day was a day of discovery as I began a lifelong love affair with the Big Apple. Ironically, in my twenties and thirties, athletics was never a priority. I ran occasionally, played tennis every now and then, but never paid much attention to physical fitness.

Shortly after I arrived in New York, the world heavyweight championship fight between Muhammad Ali and George Foreman took place. It was 1974. I paid about $30 to go to a

movie theater to watch the fight. Ali was a significant underdog, and everyone expected Foreman to kill him. Ali was the
ultimate promoter, and displayed a confidence before and during the match that made an impression on me. Ali was clearly
boxing a bigger man, a stronger man, and a man who probably
should have won the fight. But Ali beat George Foreman mentally—totally psyched him out with his fearless antics and
cockiness, both before and during the fight. Ali spoke to him
during the fight, taunting him. In short, Ali beat Foreman by
simply being Ali. In addition to his incredible will to win, it was
his spirit and charisma that beat Foreman. In addition, he had
the physical skills and boxing ability to pull it off. This was a
triumphant moment for boxing, and I reveled in Ali's glory.
The crowd at the private showing in the movie theater went
absolutely wild. I still felt a twinge every time I got close to
boxing. I knew instinctively I had a connection there; I just
didn't know what it was.

My father became ill, and I felt I should be closer to my
mother, so I moved to Dallas, still continuing in the banking
business. My father died, and I was glad I had made the move
to Texas to be nearer to my mother. Mother and I both took
his death very hard—she had taken close care of him 24 hours
a day for the last few years of his life. This experience had
established a particularly strong bond between them. His death
upset me to my core, as I realized how much his strong, silent
presence in my life had meant to me, and how he could never
really be replaced. With his death, the chapter of my childhood
connection to boxing had also been closed.

I eventually got into real estate investment banking. As
the Texas economy was crumbling in the late 1980s, I
returned to New York City as a Partner in Corporate
Finance with the now defunct Drexel Burnham, dealing
with institutional investors from all over the world. Working
on Wall Street in the late eighties was great, and I was truly
feeling like a "master of the universe," the term for Wall

Street professionals coined by Tom Wolfe in his book, *Bonfire of the Vanities*. After Drexel went bankrupt, I landed a big job with Cushman & Wakefield, as the Managing Director in charge of the firm's business nationally with financial institutions. Despite the problems of the real estate industry at that time, I had three good years with Cushman & Wakefield, including some great international experience.

As the 1990s evolved, I found a need to make some changes. After many tough but rewarding years in real estate investment banking, I made a tactical move professionally, and shifted to the money management business. In 1992, I joined Sanford C. Bernstein & Company, and became a Principal on the money management side of the firm, which is now named Bernstein Investment Research and Management. The 1990s were a great era for the stock market, and the firm did very well. I bought a fantastic apartment on 57th Street, right across the street from Carnegie Hall. I have always said that my greatest claim to fame is to be able to sit in my bed at night, look down my long hallway, through the entry way, through my dining room, through my *toes*, and see Carnegie Hall. For a guy from Pecos, Texas, that's as good as it gets.

Quietly, I was keeping an eye on the world of boxing. Next to Las Vegas, New York City is perhaps the boxing mecca of the world. There is a glorious boxing history here, and many of the best fighters of the twentieth century have called it home, including Jack Dempsey, Rocky Marciano, Joe Louis, Rocky Graziano, and Jake LaMotta. The old boxing clubs in New York City were the scene of some great fights in the first part of the twentieth century. As mentioned previously, the renowned artist George Bellows recorded the fight *Dempsey versus Firpo*, a depiction of Jack Dempsey being knocked out of the ring by Luis Angel Firpo of Argentina at Sharkey's Boxing Club on the West Side of Manhattan on September 14, 1923. The two fights between Joe Louis and Max Schmeling at Yankee Stadium leading up to World War II reached mythic status. Some of the old fight nights at

Madison Square Garden were legendary. It was at Madison Square Garden where Muhammad Ali and Joe Frazier gained boxing immortality in 1971. Both undefeated at the time, Frazier won a 15-round decision in one of the greatest, hardest hitting matches of all time.

Although I wasn't involved with the sport at the time, boxing and boxing-related activities remained very important to me. I had learned a lot from them, and regretted that I did not start boxing competitively during my youth. I wish I could have found a way to compete in the Golden Gloves. I wish I had boxed in the army. Why I didn't follow up on my father's important introduction to the sport is something I truly regret about my life. I missed out on the best years of my life for the sport. But little did I know that a white collar boxing career was still within my reach.

CHAPTER

4

ENTERING THE RING

The only true failure would be not to explore at all.
—SIR ERNEST SHACKLETON, ANTARCTIC EXPLORER

I moved to New York for the second time in 1987. Having been a real estate investment banker for several years, I had watched the Texas economy implode as the economy sank into the doldrums with the decline in real estate and oil prices. I missed New York and had always wanted to return anyway. This seemed like an appropriate time to do so. For the first few years, I had no organized program of athletics, but it was great to be back in New York. I was so busy taking advantage of the many wonderful diversions New York had to offer, physical fitness just didn't seem such a priority.

The year before I moved, I had read about a Wall Street Charity Fund Bout at Madison Square Garden's Felt Forum. One of the many fights covered in a *Time* magazine article describing the event was the heavyweight fight of Tom "The Bomb" Gimbel, a member of the New York Athletic Club Boxing Team, who was with Smith Barney at the time. The article also profiled an insurance magnate by the name of David Lawrence, who talked about how he had found his way to Gleason's Gym and then into this huge event. As mentioned previously, Lawrence went on to fight the first ever white collar sparring match in 1988. The article described the bouts of both Gimbel and Lawrence in great detail, with Gimbel having scored the only knockout of the night over his opponent. The article spoke of Lawrence's rigorous training regimen at Gleason's Gym, and how he had gotten himself in shape around the age of 40. Although Lawrence lost his bout at these fights, the article painted a great picture of getting in shape by boxing, and described the favorable changes which had occurred in Lawrence's life because of boxing. This article resonated with me, and I kept a copy of it. Here were a couple of boxers whom I could very much relate to—a couple of Wall Street guys!

In 1989, I had a business lunch to discuss a real estate deal with an investment banker by the name of Tom Gimbel. Halfway through the lunch I realized he was Tom "the Bomb." During that lunch, Tom and I talked about boxing the entire time. I learned that in addition to having a record of 29–3 as an amateur boxer, at that time he was the heavyweight champion of the New York Athletic Club (NYAC). In fact, the only fights he had lost were at the finals of the Empire State Games, the quarter finals of the Golden Gloves, and one fight against another heavyweight champion of the NYAC, Mike Fullam. Tom is a great guy and a respected pro on Wall Street, and he boxed. After our meeting, I started to wonder. Why couldn't I do this?

In the early 1990s, as I crept over the "big 4-0" and was slipping into middle age, I found myself getting "soft." Working out wasn't as much fun as it used to be. I had gained weight. My hair was turning grey. I was starting to feel old. In 1992, as part of a larger program that involved both professional and personal transformation, I made a conscious decision to jump start my athletic career. I decided to take up two sports, and, to simplify things, they were to have the following important criteria: 1) be great exercise, and 2) be fun. I thought long and hard about what those two sports should be. I thought to myself, "Is this the time to make my move into boxing?" "Well," I said to myself, "it's probably now or never!" I took up boxing and basketball with a passion in 1992. My criteria were met soundly by both sports.

Taking up boxing over the age of 40 is not something that a lot of people have done. Boxing is the only sport in the Olympics that has an age limit. That limit is 34. So I will never be an Olympic boxer. There is a reason for this—it is a tough and demanding sport. It is a sport with a lot of pain. A boxer is required to administer and receive pain on a regular basis. As the body gets older, even in your thirties, it gets harder for the body to receive pain.

I joined the NYAC in August of 1992, and found my way to the boxing room in September of that year. I looked around the room. It was a classic boxing room—high ceilings, wood paneling, two big rings, lots of bags—heavy bags, speed bags. It was the most interesting room in the NYAC, reminiscent of another era. On the walls, pictures of some of the great NYAC fighters, including Tom Gimbel and Mike Fullam, as well as the twin brothers, Nick and Pete Spanakos, who together won 17 national, regional, and local Golden Gloves titles and some 200 amateur fights each. Nick was Muhammad Ali's room-mate in the 1960 Olympics. There were also a lot of photos of boxing events that have occurred over the past few years at the NYAC, giving the room a great sense of history and continuity. It was the setting that you imagined for old time club fighting. It was a thrilling space, a space I wanted to come back to.

With all due respect to fine athletic clubs all over the world, the New York Athletic Club is probably the greatest club of its type anywhere, a veritable institution of athletics and camaraderie. It has superior facilities; a wide variety of sports and athletics; a great history, including members who have won over 214 medals in the Olympic Games (123 of which are gold) as of the spring of 2005; a terrific and dedicated staff; and an ideal location in the heart of Manhattan on Central Park South (one block from my apartment, I might add). The facility has 26 floors, a wonderful full-floor gymnasium, a great swimming pool, lots of squash courts, and, yes, a great boxing room. It has world class athletes in several sports, and always sends a healthy contingent to the Olympics to compete every four years. There is also plenty of room for anyone who simply wants to get a workout and enjoy the benefits of physical fitness. In the summer, it has a separate facility about 30 minutes north of Manhattan, near Pelham, New York, at Travers Island, which for all practical purposes is a country club with a great pool and 18 tennis courts. Joining the New York Athletic Club was one of the truly great things I have been able to do in my life.

When it was established in 1868, the NYAC's members participated in three principal sports—track and field, swimming, and boxing. These were the three prominent sports of the era. Boxing was a very popular sport, and it was quite common for young NYAC boxers not only to train together, but also to room together.

The NYAC has always taken a leadership position of organizing and sponsoring national and international championships in many sports. In 1871, just three years after the club was formed, the NYAC hosted the first-ever boxing bouts for U.S. amateur titles at the Booth Theater in Manhattan. In front of a large and enthusiastic crowd, it was a NYAC founder, Harry Beuremyer, who captured the heavyweight championship.

As the nineteenth century progressed, the athletic club movement was part of a general trend towards a more obvious demonstration and affirmation of wealth and success by the

upper class. The NYAC became the prototype for elite sporting organizations, and some of America's wealthiest and most
powerful men were counted in its membership ranks. This
movement was accompanied by a strong general upsurge of
interest in male physicality, as the popular press of the day
began to promote the idea that there was a strong link
between a man's physique and success in business.
Competitive athletics was thought to lead to forceful action in
the business world. Other sports promoted an amateur ideal,
and built clubs to help frame social exclusivity in sports like
yachting, polo, and track.

In 1884, the NYAC hired as boxing coach "Iron Mike"
Donovan, a 160-pound middleweight who was considered
one of the greatest boxers in the world and held the middleweight championship title for many years. The move to
hire Donovan was further evidence of the role of the NYAC
as an amateur boxing stronghold during that era. Donovan was
amazingly connected in the sport of boxing, and used it to
introduce himself to a broad cross-section of society. On one
occasion when Donovan fought for the middleweight championship, the match was refereed by none other than Wyatt
Earp, the famous desert lawman and adventurer, best known
with his brothers and Doc Holliday for having prevailed
against the Clanton gang at the legendary "Gunfight at the
OK Corral." Donovan was a puncher who could hold his own
with the world heavyweight champion, the "Great John L."
Sullivan, with whom he fought at least two exhibitions, even
thought Sullivan outweighed him by 30 pounds at the time.
"Iron Mike" was President Theodore Roosevelt's boxing
instructor and White House sparring partner, and was present
at many White House functions as a close friend of the president. Donovan was also a close friend of "Gentleman" Jim
Corbett, who succeeded John L. Sullivan as heavyweight
champion of the world in 1892. Mike Donovan remained
boxing coach at the NYAC well into the twentieth century

and a dynasty was created when he was followed as boxing coach by his son, Arthur. Also a leading middleweight boxer, Arthur was a highly regarded referee, who was the "third man in the ring" for many of Joe Louis' championship fights in the 1930s and 1940s.

History has helped shape the NYAC Boxing Club of today, which was officially formed in 1981. Over the past 25 years, NYAC boxers have competed in the Golden Gloves, college boxing, Empire State Games, and Olympic trials. With about 100 members, the NYAC Boxing Club is very active and presents boxing events on a regular schedule with a variety of scheduled competitions. In previous years, the NYAC Boxing Club battled teams from leading colleges, such as West Point, Penn State, and Lock Haven. For a number of years, a strong rivalry existed between the NYAC Boxing Team and the Downtown Athletic Club Boxing Team; the two clubs enjoyed many good competitions. Matches have been held with other boxing gyms around the city, including Gleason's Gym and the Trinity Boxing Club, a club located downtown near the Wall Street financial district. More recently, the NYAC Boxing Team has enjoyed a healthy rivalry with teams from the New York Police Department.

The NYAC Boxing Team has experienced and dedicated coaches and trainers, including Mike Fullam, former NYAC heavyweight champion, and Dan O'Leary, former head coach of the New York Police Department Boxing Team. Sitting on the NYAC Boxing Committee is Hall of Fame boxing referee Arthur Mercante, who can often be heard announcing NYAC fight competitions. Arthur Mercante retired as a professional boxing referee in 2003, having officiated at over 120 world championship fights. Some of the fights for which he served as "third man in the ring" are legendary, and include the first Ali–Frazer world heavyweight championship fight at Madison Square Garden in 1971 and the Foreman–Frazer world heavyweight championship fight in 1973. Today, Arthur is a very active member of the NYAC Boxing Club. His son, Arthur, Jr., also a member of the NYAC, is a leading professional boxing referee too.

I heard the boxing team worked out on Tuesday nights, so I timidly went in there one September night in 1992. I was greeted by Ronnie Cecchetti, who was the NYAC head boxing coach at that time. Ronnie was an ex-pro, and a very patient trainer. He began to work with me during my appearances in the boxing room. I worked out on the bags, jumping rope, shadow boxing, training with mitts, weight training, running ("roadwork"), and general conditioning for at least nine months. I remember my first attempts at the footwork which is so necessary for a boxer, and is made to look easy by the professionals I was used to watching. At first, I found it extremely difficult to move in the crab-like manner, shuffling my feet forward, backward, and to the side, which is fundamental to the movement necessary for a boxer to maintain the proper balance and be prepared to throw and receive punches. I have never had great balance, and found this foot movement one of the hardest routines to adapt to.

Things were going okay, and my confidence began to rise as I went through the various drills and training exercises. Finally, Ronnie thought it was time for me to try sparring. In essence, sparring is supervised boxing. It is designed to give boxers a way to practice the sport in a highly supervised environment, with a trainer on the side of the ring at all times. However, punches are thrown hard, and it is, for all practical purposes, fighting. Because it is meant to be instructive, the referee or trainer can stop the sparring session at will to give either or both fighters pointers, or let them rest if necessary.

I had no idea what to expect my first time sparring. I had hit the heavy bag so many times, I felt I had put my own personal dent in it. I was getting so good on the speed bag I could do it with rapid fire precision. I was feeling good about this sport, and looking forward to taking it to the next level. One Saturday morning, Ronnie had arranged for me to spar with Nick "The Tank" Mahoney, a NYAC boxer I had seen working out in the boxing room from time to time. Nick had become a friend, but was a very serious, mean-looking guy in the ring. I wondered what kind of experience this would be. I remember feeling flattered that Ronnie thought I was good enough to spar, as sparring in many ways is just like fighting, and a fighter has to be in great shape to even try it.

I climbed in the ring that day rested and relaxed. Ronnie had put on my hand wraps, gloves, and headgear. I had bought a mouthpiece a few days earlier, which was required for sparring, and had shaped it to the size of my mouth the night before. This process requires boiling it in water for a specified period of time, and then putting it into your mouth while it is pliable, and shaping it around your teeth. Ronnie explained the rules: we would spar three, three-minute rounds, with one minute between each round. So it was nine minutes of sparring, with two minutes to rest, in total. Ronnie suggested we take it easy, at least to begin with, and "work with each other." The term "work with each other" suggests a sparring session in which the two boxers get a good workout and punch hard, but without the intensity of a competitive match, in which each boxer is usually trying to take the other guy's head off.

The bell rang, and Nick started walking toward me. All of a sudden, he did not look like Nick—he looked like this big, ugly, menacing force, heading straight for me and about to start swinging for my head. The thought of this made my knees weak. I backpedaled. My heart rate accelerated, and I began heaving to get my breath. I realized that I was hyperventilating. Before either of us could throw a punch, I waved to Ronnie to stop the exercise, as I was really in a state of panic! Ronnie called a halt to Nick, and Nick immediately backed off while Ronnie calmed me down and I got my breath. I was greatly relieved, but my confidence was badly shaken.

After that, we went on to "work with each other" for three light rounds. I managed to get through it and survive. But my confidence had been shattered. That's when I realized another truth about boxing. You can be in excellent physical shape, look in superb condition in the gym, do everything right with the bags and shadow boxing—but actual boxing, or sparring, is a whole other story. Sparring is what "separates the men from the boys" in the boxing room. I went back to the drawing boards, and it was another month before I had the courage to try sparring again.

I continued to come up to the boxing room on Tuesday nights, and did my routine—bags, rope, shadow boxing, ring movement—and worked with Ronnie on the mitts. I shied away from sparring for a while. Finally, I got involved in a "round robin" one evening. A round robin is where three or four fighters rotate in and out of the boxing ring, as two fighters spar at all times. Usually, if there are four fighters, one fighter will spar one round with each of the three other fighters, then that fighter will rotate out, and the last fighter he sparred with will stay in for two more rounds with each of the other two fighters. It keeps going in that rotating process until everyone has had a good workout.

I managed to get through one of these sessions, with the guys going pretty easy on me. It was a truly exhilarating exercise. It was also extremely intense. While sparring, a fighter has to use so many physical resources all at once. A fighter has to be in great shape, have great endurance, be able to hold his or her arms up for extended periods of time— try it some time!—and be able to handle the intensity of looking directly at someone who is doing everything they can to hurt you. It's hard to understand how much physical stamina this requires unless you've done it. It is like no other sport I know; it simply takes everything you have, physically and mentally, to do it right.

The mental part is worth mentioning. At least 50 percent of the sport is psychological. A fighter has to have confidence that he has the skill, the stamina, and the necessary training to stand up to an opponent. Why was Ali able to beat George Foreman, a younger, stronger, and bigger man? Because he had confidence in himself and his ability. This same phenomenon exists on an amateur or white collar level. Ali took the confidence game to an extreme, famously taunting his opponents to try to psych them out before a fight.

One thing a boxer learns early in his career is that size and strength are not what matters the most. I have seen many a smaller man pummel a larger man. I have seen muscle-bound guys get trounced by "average"-looking boxers. What matters is how prepared a boxer is—mentally and physically. What also matters is one fighter's ability to "relax" in the ring and concentrate on the job at hand, without being distracted by the physical intensity or the attempts by the opponent to inflict physical pain.

The word "relax" has a special meaning in boxing. It means the ability to be in the throes of competition, surrounded by all of that intensity, and to keep your wits about you, keep your body loose and agile, not tense up and lose your composure. I was initially fooled by this word when my trainers first used it, as I think of relaxing as taking a nap on a Saturday afternoon at the beach, or watching television in my apartment at the end of a hard day at the office. Relaxing in the ring is one of the most important things a boxer can do, and an important concept to master. There are volumes written about this subject, and many others relating to the martial arts and self defense. One great writer on the martial arts was Bruce Lee, perhaps the greatest martial artist of all time, and I recommend his works highly. However, in the early phase of my boxing career, I was unfamiliar with the teachings of Bruce Lee. I would discover them at a later date, and they would change completely the way I approached boxing.

Somewhere in the summer or early fall of 1993, I was in a round-robin session with some of the NYAC boxing team members. I had advanced somewhat, but the guys were still taking it pretty easy on me, I could tell. I was anxious to improve my boxing, and really wanted to be just another one of the guys on the team. One evening I was sparring with Chris "Whiplash" Angle, a light heavyweight around 170 pounds. Chris is a great athlete. Around 40 at the time, he had several years of experience in boxing, and was an extremely good judo player. Chris would work out with the boxing team for over an hour, and then do another hour in the judo room. He could spar for 10 to 12 rounds easily, and was in remarkable physical condition. He was polite to me, but I could tell that he had no respect for me as a boxer. He sparred with me, nevertheless, out of courtesy.

Then one day, it happened. I was sparring with Chris Angle, and I hit him. I really tagged him! He looked stunned. He said something unintelligible to me—I think it was "good punch." I could tell that his intensity changed. He started moving differently in the ring with me. In boxing "ring language," he was beginning to treat me with respect. It was a great moment for me. I started really sparring with a lot of the guys, taking on anyone who would get in the ring with me. I had finally "arrived" at the NYAC boxing room.

From that point on, I really began to enjoy the sport. I trained all the time, working with anyone who appeared in the ring before me. I felt I was getting better, gaining confidence. I actually gave Nick Mahoney a black eye in one of our sparring sessions. In short, I was overcoming my fears. But was it premature?

CHAPTER

5

MY FIRST
FIGHT NIGHTS

You miss 100% of the shots you never take.
—WAYNE GRETSKY, HOCKEY PLAYER

In September of 1993, Ronnie Cecchetti made an announcement—the New York Athletic Club was going to host the 125th Club Anniversary Bouts. This was a club boxing championship, commemorating the 125th anniversary of the NYAC. I thought to myself, could I possibly enter? I wasn't sure I was ready. But, then, when would I ever be really ready? I had been sparring for several months. I was in good shape. I assumed they would not put me in with someone who would kill me. So I signed up, and continued to train very hard. Although I did not know quite what to expect, I knew this event would not be just another sparring session. I knew there would be a live audience, which would mean added pressure and intensity. I would be competing for the New York Athletic Boxing Team for the first time. I went through my various routines with a renewed seriousness, and sparred at every chance I got. Still, I had no real idea how serious the upcoming contest would actually be.

A couple weeks before the bouts, which were held on October 25, 1993, I learned that I was going to fight Scott "Slick" Butler. Scott Butler was someone I had known at Drexel Burnham. He was a big man, 220-plus pounds, an inch or two shorter than me. I was weighing around 200 to 205, which is what I have weighed for many years now. He was ten years younger than me, and a decent boxer. We had sparred together some, and were pretty well matched, I thought. The fights were to be held in the boxing room of the NYAC.

Finally, the night of the fights arrived. I invited friends to attend. A bar was set up in the boxing room. People were drinking, smoking. It was a boxing club "scene." It was exciting!

Earlier in the week, Ronnie Cecchetti had asked me for my "handle." A handle in boxing is a name a fighter is known by. Throughout history, boxers like "Iron" Mike Tyson and Evander "The Real Deal" Holyfield have had handles. I'm not sure exactly why. Even many of the old English boxers—such as Jem Belcher "Napoleon of the Ring," Henry Pearce "The Game Chicken," and Tom Cribb "The Black Diamond"—had them. I think it adds great interest to the sport, and is another thing that makes it unique. I had not thought about this, but I instinctively told him, "I'm The Pecos Kid." Pecos, Texas was my hometown, my roots. It is unique place, with a unique name. That night I became John "The Pecos Kid" Oden. It's my handle to this very day.

Not knowing what to expect, and being a bit naïve about the mental preparation necessary for a fight, I got into my dress uniform and wandered down to the boxing room about an hour before the fights began, where my friends were beginning to gather. Being social by nature, I really enjoyed seeing everyone and the uniqueness of the occasion. After this first fight, though, I came to appreciate the intense mental preparation necessary and this socializing before a fight was an experience I was never to repeat. I attach a write-up from *The*

Introducing John "The Pecos Kid" Oden

Winged Foot, the monthly magazine of the NYAC, which described our fight that night:

> *The 125th Anniversary bouts began with John "Pecos Kid" Oden going toe-to-toe with Scott "Slick" Butler. Both fighters were competing in their first bout. Butler took the first round by counter-punching Oden whenever John missed with his lethal Texas-Cobra right. In a sparring session in preparation for the bouts this Oden weapon left its mark on the eye of Nick "The Tank" Mahoney. In later rounds Oden impressed the judges by landing the heavier blows and receiving the nod over the eager Butler who had trouble with John's wing-span, which on most fighters is referred to as "a reach."*

It was over so fast, I couldn't believe it. I had won! My friends were ecstatic. I was in total disbelief. While I had not known what to expect, I was thrilled with the experience. My friend Leigh Curry was so excited, he followed me back to the locker room afterwards, talking about the fight non-stop. I could hardly go to sleep that night. And I received a huge trophy. I was hooked on the sport, but not exactly sure where I'd go from there.

One other thing that resonated with me that night was the appearance of Jack Kendrick as a last-minute substitution for someone who did not show up to fight at the middleweight level. Jack was in his late fifties at the time, and literally rose from the crowd with no notice whatsoever, and got in the ring to fight. Jack Kendrick, who was later to become one of my trainers and closest friends, is a world-class athelete who has taught boxing and track and field all over the world. He fought well, and moved like a rabbit. I later learned that his boxing handle is "The Dancing Ghost," which I thought was a most appropriate name for him, given his speed. I was impressed that he was able to fight at the spur of the moment.

In the next issue of *Sports Illustrated*, the magazine made a brief statement about the bouts, and mentioned that Jack Kendrick had emerged in the boxing world again at the 125th NYAC Anniversary Bouts to win the NYAC's middleweight title. I had fought the only true heavyweight fight of the night, but there was no mention of John Oden winning the heavyweight title! In fact, I never considered that I won this title. There were certainly better heavyweights in the club at the time; mine was a first-time fight for me and I had been matched accordingly. There are those who have referred to me as the heavyweight champ ever since, and I am grateful to those people, but there is no doubt that if a heavyweight contest were held at the NYAC, then or now, I would not be the last man standing.

White collar boxing uses amateur boxing weight classes, which are somewhat different than professional classes. Matchups in white collar boxing are made by both weight and ability, with ability being the more important of the two. Sometimes opponents from different weight classes are matched together, if they are thought by the coaching staffs to be of similar overall ability. Age is also a factor. Today the weight classes are set by establishing the maximum number of pounds in each class. The 178-pound class or the 201-pound class means that the fighter in that class can weigh no more than that weight. At the time of the Anniversary Bouts, though, in 1993, anyone weighing over 190 pounds was classified as a heavyweight; I weighed in at 200 pounds.

I kept my weekly sparring workouts, supplemented on other days by weight training and running. I kept in decent shape. Then, in February of 1995, the NYAC announced a competitive fight night with the Downtown Athletic Club. The Downtown Athletic Club was another athletic institution in New York. It was home of the annual dinner to award the Heismann trophy, which is given to the best college football player each year. I had been to this dinner and awards ceremony once, when Earl Campbell of the University of Texas was awarded the trophy in 1977; I was President of the University of Texas Alumni Association of New York (the "Texas Exes") at the time. A fight against the Downtown Athletic Club was a big time event! I had come a long way in my boxing career, but I was not sure I was ready to throw myself into that arena and did not plan to participate.

A few days later, I got a call from Ronnie Cecchetti, who said he had something for me to advance my career. I said, "Ronnie, what do you mean—advance my career?" Ronnie said, "I mean your boxing career!" He went on to tell me that he wanted me to fight John Turco, who was the chairman of the Downtown Athletic Club Boxing Team. John was about my age, supposedly a great guy, and on the Board of Governors at the Downtown Athletic Club. The Downtown Athletic Club (DAC) really wanted a match for John, and everyone involved thought I would be the man for the job. After some thought, I agreed, but the thought of getting into the ring with someone I had never met was a bit daunting. I trained hard for the match.

Finally, on April 19, 1995, the big event arrived. Again, it was held in the NYAC boxing room. Because John was such an important person at the DAC and because we were both heavyweights, we were billed as the main event. In boxing, the main event is usually the last bout of the night, and the most important bout of the night. When world champions fight professionally, there is usually a "card" of several fights for the evening, with the championship or main event fight being the last. Everyone waits for the main event with great anticipation.

I met John Turco in the NYAC locker room the night of the fight. He is an extremely affable guy, an electrical contractor who had recently taken up boxing and had been a member of the DAC for years. He told me that his main sport was golf, and that he was just trying to get through the fight that night without embarrassing himself. My confidence grew.

Finally, it was time for our bout. The house was packed. It was a rowdy crowd, and this was the match many of them had come for. There were a lot of supporters for John Turco. I had several friends and people from my office there, as well.

John Turco and I were announced, and there was much cheering. Turco's handle was "The Torturer." *The Torturer,* I thought to myself. The bell rang, and "The Torturer" came out swinging. He was trying to take my head off! I danced out of his way time and again. He was really coming after me. I couldn't believe it. What happened to the nice guy I met in the locker room?

The first two rounds were pretty even. Turco swung a lot, and missed a lot. He never really connected with me. I kept moving and jabbing, just staying out of his way. Then the bell rang for the third round. I moved quickly. I delivered to Turco one of the best combinations I have ever thrown. A combination is a classic one-two punch, where you lead with your jab (which is my left hand) and then come across with a strong, straight, right-hand punch. Combinations are considered the most effective way to inflict pain and wear down an opponent. I threw a great combination to Turco. My left backed him up. I then moved forward to deliver the straight right, which connected straight on. Down he went! Turco finished the round on his back. I couldn't believe it. Turco sat there on the floor blinking for a few seconds, and was attempting to get up, when the bell rang. It seemed to me that the bell had been rung early. Others later agreed. I knew I had won the fight!

We went to the center of the ring for the announcer (the famous professional referee, Arthur Mercante, Sr.) to call out the winner. I was waiting to raise my hand, when the fight was announced as a draw. A draw! How could this fight be a draw? I did not protest, but I felt robbed. I learned another lesson about boxing—politics plays an important role, even on the amateur or white collar level. In my opinion, Turco was such an important person at the DAC, political influence was exerted so that a "draw" could be rendered and not embarrass him and, at the same time, encourage him to continue to box.

After the fight, everyone congratulated me as if I had won. People acknowledged that I should have gotten the decision, but I was still a little stunned that it was called a draw. However, when I thought about it, it really wasn't that big of a deal. It was just a surprising decision. *The Winged Foot* of the New York Athletic Club reported the fight thusly:

> *The eighth bout found stocky tyro John Turco, a Governor of the DAC, making a very game, aggressive try against former NYAC Heavyweight Champ John Oden, an imposing 6'4", 205 lbs. with a dangerous long hard right hand which he frequently uses for counter-punching. Turco pressed the fight from the bell and gave Oden little breathing room or opportunity to take control of the bout. By the last round, though, Oden's punches were finding their target and he decked Turco with a left-right combo just before the final bell. In amateur boxing a knockdown counts as only one punch in the scoring and cannot be given undue weight by the judges. As a result the bout was called a draw.*

Turco and I developed a good relationship, and were to meet two more times in the ring. The next time was on October 23, 1995, at the NYAC versus DAC boxing matches, which were held at the DAC. Ronnie Cecchetti had approached me to fight a rematch with Turco on the home court of the DAC, which I had agreed to do. It was a difficult time for me, however, as my mother, Violet, who was 93 and had been living with me in my apartment for the past two years, was very ill. Three weeks before the fight, she died, and I went to Pecos, Texas, to take care of the arrangements for her funeral. I was out of training for a week, and really thrown off mentally.

Nevertheless, once I commit to something, I commit to it. The night of the big fight arrived. In later years, having a huge entourage was to become a trademark of mine. That night, due to the circumstances leading up to the fight, I had only three or four close friends with me.

The room chosen for the fight was a small gymnasium, much bigger than the boxing room at the NYAC, and it was packed. There was an open bar in one corner. Lots of cigar smoke. It was an extremely rowdy crowd, and Turco was the king! Turco was cheered and idolized by these people. When I was announced, I was booed loudly. I envisioned the crowd throwing lettuce and tomatoes at me, the booing was so fierce. There was little or no turnout from the NYAC. And I had heard while still in the dressing room that "Smokin' Joe" Frazier was in the audience that night. Not only was I in a hostile atmosphere, underprepared, but the former Heavyweight Champion of the World was here to watch me fight. Now, that's pressure!

Again, Turco and I were scheduled for the main event. The bell rang and off we went. Turco was much improved from our first fight. He was in good shape, delivering much more effective punches. My mother's death had been a big setback to my training. I was not there mentally, the way I should have been. And Turco was loaded for bear. I knew my boxing moves that night were not polished. At the end of the second round, he hit me with a very hard shot. Between rounds, Vinnie Ferguson, a NYAC referee and former boxing Olympian who was refereeing the fight, came over to my corner and said to Ronnie Cecchetti, "Your man took a hard shot at the end of the round, is he okay?" Ronnie and I assured him I was. In the meantime, the crowd was going wild! I'd never seen such a rowdy crowd. They were restless—drinking and smoking and having a great time. There was electricity in the room.

The bell rang at the end of the third round, signaling the end of the fight. I had a sense that I had lost the fight. Waiting for the announcer to announce the decision, I was not surprised when Turco's hand was raised. "Smokin' Joe" Frazier gave me my medal, and whispered in my ear that I had done a good job. I appreciated his saying that, more than he will ever know. I congratulated Turco, and went to the showers. I had never lost before—no matter that my mother had just died, no matter that my training had been interrupted, it was a creepy feeling. I learned that I did not like to lose! I knew I had not fought up to my potential. For that I had a bit of a sheepish feeling as I mixed and mingled with the crowd that gathered at the bar afterwards. Yes, I had personal problems, but most of the crowd didn't know that; as far as they were concerned, I had just lost. I determined never to go into the ring underprepared again. My feelings did not completely diminish the magic of the moment, but I would have enjoyed the aftermath even more had I been victorious that night, or at least have been able to give it my all.

Turco and I were to meet one more time. A "rubber match" was scheduled for October 23, 1996. A rubber match is when two fighters have fought twice, and each has won one. One of the classic rubber matches in boxing history was the final fight between Muhammad Ali and Joe Frazier. Each fighter had won one fight, and a rubber match was called for, as there was something yet to be decided. When Ali won the third fight, he became the winner of the rubber match, the series, and the long-term victor. In the case of Joe Louis and Max Schmeling, there was no need for a third match, or rubber match, because Louis had destroyed Schmeling in the first round of the second match. I truly believe people referred to my third match with Turco as a rubber match because those who were there were convinced that I had won that first fight with Turco. Clearly, he had won the second. There was actually a fair amount of interest in this third fight, despite my poor showing in the second. I decided to go all out to win.

The rubber match between John Turco and me was part of a NYAC–DAC challenge. Again, our fight was slated for the main event. It was again held at the DAC, and I was mentally prepared for the rowdy, bawdy atmosphere of their boxing facility this time. This time I brought an entourage, which consisted of about 20 people. John Turco had met us when we arrived, and could not have been nicer to me and my group. He was as genuinely hospitable as he could be, a true gentleman. However, in the ring, it was another matter.

For the Turco–Oden rubber match, I had asked to be trained by both Ronnie Cecchetti and Jack Kendrick. I wanted all of the help I could get. I had developed a special relationship with both of these men, and I had a terrific time getting prepared for this match.

I also learned what a special guy Jack "The Dancing Ghost" Kendrick is. Jack is a world class athlete who has competed and coached boxing, and track and field, all over the world. He was the middleweight champion at the University of Dublin, and won boxing titles in the U.S. Army in France, Austria, and Kenya. He was in the Olympic Trials in track in 1956. Since his heyday as an amateur in both boxing and track and field, he has stayed close to athletics as a coach and trainer.

Jack Kendrick is also a true renaissance man. Professionally, he is an actor and a poet. He has appeared in five movies, and has acted regularly in many daily soap operas, including "Another World," and "Love Is a Many Splendored Thing." He has been awarded two Rockefeller Grants for poetry and drama. Even more impressive is that he travels all over the world, to leading colleges and universities, reading his own poetry. This is how he makes his living. I don't know anyone quite like him. He is also truly a sincere and decent man, who is an inspirational coach and trainer. Jack Kendrick has helped me be a better boxer. He has also helped me be a better man.

Just before the fight, I was relaxing in the locker room, getting myself mentally prepared for the fight. For me, this meant lying down, and relaxing, thinking over my fight plan, and making sure my equipment was in order. Jack Kendrick came over to see me, and give me some encouraging words. He has a way of taking the edge off of any situation. I appreciated his kind words. About 30 minutes before fight time, he placed the following letter in my hand:

> John,
>
> *There's so much missed in this world by people who have a reluctance to "put things on the line" in reality—rather only experiencing those victories and defeats vicariously—either as a spectator, or by way of movies, TV or magazines. You are one of the few who go into the furnace of competition and for this, you are a rare, and fortunate, human being. Therefore, whether the outcome be victory or defeat, you have already won. I am proud of your efforts, and I am honored to have shared your effort.*
>
> *Jack Kendrick*

I was deeply touched by his words. They were truly inspirational to me. I read them a couple of times, and then put them in my locker as I continued my preparation for the fight. But I was blown away by Jack Kendrick's gesture. His letter is now framed and hanging with other of my boxing memorabilia in my apartment.

Fight time arrived, and I walked towards the ring, and climbed in it. There is nothing quite like that walk. Despite the crowds, despite the trainers and friends who might be there to support you, it is truly a lonely feeling. Standing in the ring and waiting for the fight to start is a very anxious time. It is a time when you realize what must be done in the next few minutes, and how difficult it is going to be. It gives real meaning to the cliché "moment of truth." Somehow, the crowd was a little friendlier to me this time, because I was somewhat well known at the DAC at this point, and I think they respected me. So I did not get as many boos and catcalls as I had previously.

The fight began, and Turco came at me. Things were going fine and then, all of a sudden, he tackled me. Down we went—it was a ridiculous scene. We both got up, and were boxing again. Then he tackled me again. Down we went. I couldn't believe it. Finally, things settled down, and we had a decent fight, but I always thought the two tackles by Turco in the first round threw some cold water on the impression the crowd had of the fight. He would later apologize for this, but never gave a real explanation—just nervous, I guess. I hit him with some good shots, he hit me with a couple. Overall, it was probably our best fight. I was in much better condition than I'd been for my last fight with "The Torturer." He was in good shape, too. There were no really big punches. The fight drew to a close and the final bell sounded. The judges ruled the fight a draw. This time, it probably was.

So ended the "Turco wars." John Turco became a good friend of mine along the way. In later years, we celebrated birthdays together, shared family times together, even got seats together at Cedric Kushner's Heavyweight Explosion series. In fact, I have formed good friendships with most of the people I have fought or sparred with. It is a sport that breeds great camaraderie. I count John Turco as one of my good friends today.

With the pressure of the Turco rubber match behind me, I went forward in my boxing workouts at the NYAC. Formal matches were few and far between, but the Tuesday night boxing club workouts continued, and I enjoyed just being part of the team and staying in shape. In general, I just kept "hacking away" at the sport.

CHAPTER

6

GLEASON'S GYM

*Now, whoever has courage and a strong and
collected spirit in his breast, let him come forward,
lace on the gloves, and put up his hands*

—THE POET VIRGIL, AND THE MANTRA OF GLEASON'S GYM

As 1996 drew to a close, I felt I had arrived on the NYAC fight circuit. I had made important strides forward. I had challenged myself. People knew I boxed. I was flattered when strangers would come up to me in restaurants and tell me that they had seen me fight one of the Turco fights. I had impressive trophies in my office. Things were going pretty well. The only problem was that the NYAC didn't compete that often. I actually had to miss a couple of the fights because I had professional conflicts.

One of my boxing buddies at the NYAC at that time was Bill "Hurricane" Hunnicutt. Bill is a year older than me, and in extraordinary physical condition. He is about my height (I am 6'4"), or a little taller. He works out constantly, and is in great shape. He is sculpted and strong. He has a chiseled face, and a lean, muscular frame. In short, when it comes to boxing, he looks the part. In fact, he was a very good boxer, although he has since retired from the sport.

Bill is a real athlete, having been the quarterback of his football team at Hamilton College, and a basketball player as well. He was always looking for a challenge. He had actually fought Turco twice in the competitive nights between the NYAC and the DAC, and had won one and lost one.

One day Bill came to me to let me know that he was going down to Gleason's Gym to fight in one of their white collar sparring nights. At that point, I wasn't sure what white collar sparring was. He explained it, and told me that Gleason's had a monthly show where Bruce Silverglade, the owner of Gleason's, would match up anyone for a three two-minute round sparring match—there was no winner or loser, and both participants got a trophy. This seemed intriguing to me. So I went down with Bill and his family one night when he was going to box in one of the Gleason's white collar shows. Bill had been working out there, in addition to his workouts at the NYAC, and even had a trainer at Gleason's.

I loved Gleason's Gym from the minute I walked into it. I loved the smell of it, the sounds of it, the authenticity of it. I was thrilled to be there, and to see my friend fight. I went down there with Bill two more times to watch him compete over the next several months. He did well in these fights. I admired that he could go down there and be ready to fight anyone Bruce Silverglade sent his way. This seemed to me to be the ultimate test for a boxer—being able to go to an important boxing gym like Gleason's and accept a challenge from anyone you might be matched up with. It also sent chills up my spine, knowing how tough a sport it is. But Bill did fine, and we had some great evenings together, and wonderful dinners afterwards with his family and friends.

Gleason's is a true classic, a throwback to a bygone era. It is the oldest and busiest active boxing gym in the world. When you enter, the first sound you hear is the steady tap-tap-tap-tap of someone skipping rope. Someone in another corner is rattling a speed bag. Two boxers begin sparring in the center ring, as a crowd gathers to watch. An area in the center section holds four heavy bags, which are almost always in use. Fighters dance around these as they "stick and move" with lefts and rights. Occasionally a loud thud is heard from the one ring reserved for wrestling, as someone is thrown to the canvas. Trainers are always present—most are former boxers who work at nominal rates. The quality of the trainers at Gleason's is par excellence. On one of the walls hangs a large banner with a quote from the poet Virgil written over 2000 years ago which has become the Gleason's mantra. *"Now, whoever has courage and a strong and collected spirit in his breast, let him come forward, lace on the gloves and put up his hands."* One must, indeed, have courage to enter this legendary boxing hall and lace up the gloves. Yes, Gleason's is a special place.

In the far corner is an enclosed area, which is Bruce Silverglade's office. About 100 photographs line the walls of the legendary boxers who trained there—Ali, Tyson, Roberto Duran, Jake LaMotta, Carlos Ortiz, many of them world champions. I am very proud that my photograph hangs there as well, with New York State Senator Joseph Bruno, former number one ranked heavyweight contender Gerry Cooney, and Bruce Silverglade—another story I will explain later. One hundred and thirty World Champions have called Gleason's home during its nearly seven decades in existence. In addition, many World Champions made Gleason's their home away from home, including Muhammad Ali, Vito Antuofermo, Eddie Mustafa Muhammad, Saoul Mamby, Wilfred Benitez, Pipino Costello, Mick McCallum, Hector Camacho, Livingstone Bramble, Julio Cesar Chavez, Jose L. Rosario, and Eusabio Pedroza. Larry Holmes, Michael Spinks, Thomas Hearns, Milton McCrory, and Barry McGuigan were among those champions who trained at Gleason's even though their home base was elsewhere.

When Gerry Cooney turned pro in 1977, he made Gleason's his training home. Gerry is best remembered in professional boxing for his 1982 bid against Larry Holmes for the Heavyweight Championship of the World. Although he did not succeed against the highly skilled Holmes, who held the title from 1978–1985, Gerry amassed a very enviable record of 28–3 as a professional boxer.

You can't help but feel history all around you as you enter the gym. Gleason's was founded in 1937 by Peter Robert Gagliardi, a former flyweight boxer turned bantamweight. He changed his name to Bobby Gleason to appeal to the predominantly Irish New York fight crowd of the era and opened the doors to the gym in the Bronx. In the beginning, dues were two dollars a month and times were tough. Bobby could not meet expenses, including the $50 per month rent, so he hacked a cab for 10 to 12 hours a night to help make ends meet. Things eased up after the Depression. In the 1940s and 1950s, Gleason's flourished along with boxing, but the 1960s took their toll. The sport fell into decline and two of its temples, Stillman's Gym and the old Madison Square Garden closed. That left Gleason's as the last remnant of boxing's "Golden Age" in New York City.

In 1974, and at the age of 82, Bobby Gleason pulled up his roots of 37 years in the Bronx and Gleason's moved to Manhattan at 252 West 30th Street. Gleason's was sold to businessman Ira Becker in 1981, who brought strong leadership to the gym. Bruce Silverglade became his partner and half-owner in 1983, then took early retirement from Sear's and joined the gym full-time as its sole owner in 1985. The 30th Street location went co-op in 1984, and Gleason's was forced again to find a new home. It settled in its current location in Brooklyn at 83 Front Street, directly under the Brooklyn Bridge.

The 15,000-square-foot gym is a boxer's paradise. More importantly, it draws a diverse crowd representing a true cross section of New York. It gives people concerned with physical fitness a place to go. It's also an important and affordable venue for those wanting to gain confidence and skill in the ring. Bruce Silverglade has described Gleason's as a "big community center, which draws from all walks of life in New York." For the most part, professional boxers come from the lower socioeconomic levels. Traditionally, boxing is a sport of the underclass, of the underdog. In twentieth century America, men have sometimes used boxing to fight their way out of poverty, to get out of prison, to fight their way out of hope-lessness. These people are present in the gym, as are teachers, bankers, brokers, and successful businessmen and women. It is a true melting pot, like New York City itself. Today the gym has 970 members. This includes approximately 350 amateur and professional boxers and over 600 recreational boxers, 200 of which are female.

Over the years, Gleason's has developed a reputation for its stable of great trainers. Currently the gym has almost 80 trainers, 80 to 85 percent of whom are ex-professional box-ers. The list is too long to mention, but includes many of the great ones. Trainers are available at very reasonable rates to all boxers—professional, amateur, or white collar. I have used several of them. A trainer is an extremely important compo-nent in the development of a boxer. Having high-quality trainers available to anyone who walks in the door is a huge positive. Generally, someone who works out there regularly will select one trainer, and work with that person for a long period of time.

Gleason's Gym has always exuded an aura of championship boxing. The reputation of the boxers it produced earned Gleason's Gym a position at the pinnacle of excellence in the sport. During the last decade or two, however, the gym has gained a new dimension. With the advent of white collar box-ing, investment bankers, corporate executives, fashion models, office workers, and actors can now be seen shadow boxing alongside champions. Gleason's time-honored approach to boxing training has paid off in the gym's consistent ability to attract a growing membership of not just championship hopefuls, but fitness-conscience individuals who understand the benefit of a boxing workout. This phenomenon has been underscored with the recent success of the movie *Million Dollar Baby*, and boxing has a new face to the average American family. Many people are able to see for the first time that boxing is great exercise for anyone, a terrific way to get in shape and an achievable goal. For the first time in history, boxing is now reaching the masses.

When you spend a little time at Gleason's, even as a spectator, you feel this. You will also feel the inclusion and acceptance of all who "come forward, lace on the gloves and put up their hands." All members of the gym identify with each other as fighters first and foremost—their differences fade into the background. Whether you are a man or a woman, working out as a professional, an amateur, or a white collar boxer, you are welcomed and respected.

White collar sparring was conceived and implemented by Bruce Silverglade in 1988, and I think of him as the godfather of white collar boxing. Prior to this, Bruce had held open competitive matches for scrappy, determined, non-professional, non-amateur-status individuals who nevertheless wanted to try their skill at the sweet science in a supervised setting at a boxing gym. Among others, high-powered Wall Street professionals would come to Gleason's and fight. If they won, terrific—Wall Street is a culture that worships winning. However, if they lost, the individual would sometimes get so upset that they would never try it again. Bruce lost a lot of clients over the years for this reason. He conferred with the Amateur Boxing President and the New York State Athletic Commission to organize white collar boxing on a more formal basis. When this effort was unsuccessful, Bruce established the white collar boxing program in which registered amateur boxers and professional boxers could not participate. Both participants got a trophy in order to avoid the designated "loser" having to face his friends and colleagues from work—a brilliant marketing strategy, in my view. Now, he was able to retain the highly competitive Wall Street types much longer. Bruce's business is flourishing today, and has jump-started an industry.

A white collar sparring night is held once a month at Gleason's, during which anyone who wishes to put their advancement in the sport to the test can volunteer to be matched up with someone of approximately equal experience and skill in a three-round match. I have fought in about ten of these white collar sparring nights over the years, and remember all of them vividly—it's an experience that's hard to forget. And in the ring at the start of every monthly white collar sparring night at Gleason's is Bruce Silverglade. No one has ever been more enthusiastic about a job than Bruce. He is always at Gleason's. He announces every fight and introduces every fighter. He is polished and well spoken. He handles the timing of the bell personally for every round—this, by the way, gives me great confidence as a boxer. He watches the referees carefully to make sure they are in complete command of each situation. He does all this because he feels it is too important a job to delegate—and he's right.

There is one other aspect of Gleason's that makes it interesting—it's a media haven, always has been. This is not a reason to go there, per se, just an added bonus that makes it a fun place to hang out. A day doesn't go by that Bruce Silverglade doesn't get some type of media request from somewhere in the world. Boxing is like a small family and in order to survive, it needs all the support it can get within the industry. The press is treated as a friend. Over 200 major magazines worldwide have written pieces on Gleason's Gym, in addition to thousands of newspaper articles. Almost every major television news station has had cameras in the place at one time or another. Gleason's has been the location for numerous television shows and fashion layouts. Hilary Swank put Gleason's on the radar screen of many average Americans when she acknowledged the gym and its trainers when she accepted her Best Actress Academy Award for *Million Dollar Baby.* Other famous actors have trained for major Hollywood movies there—Robert DeNiro for *Raging Bull* and Wesley Snipes for *Streets of Gold,* just to mention two.

And there is nothing more exciting for a boxing fan than to be at Gleason's on a Saturday morning before a big professional fight takes place. Boxing has always been a sport that thrives on debate and controversy. Gleason's is no exception. The boxing gossip and the predictions are flying. "Is Gatti ready for this one?" "Did Evander Holyfield train properly?" "Can Roy Jones, Jr., handle the weight loss?" Participating in the buzz are anyone and everyone who will listen. It is fun to hear a professional boxer make such predictions, for example, about what he thinks might happen that night in a big fight at Madison Square Garden.

It is under this backdrop of professional boxing excellence and serious training that white collar boxing was founded and now flourishes. From my perspective, as a seasoned white collar boxer, I appreciate this atmosphere which Gleason's provides, as it makes the sport more interesting to me. You never know the background of another boxer you might meet at Gleason's Gym. And some of my best friendships have been formed there. There is something very special about having participated with someone in a white collar sparring match, even though you were trying to take their head off at the time—it is a very special bonding.

In the fall of 1997, I decided I wanted to fight in one of Gleason's white collar shows, and approached Bruce Silverglade about making it a NYAC versus Gleason's Gym fight night. He was all for it. I managed to get five or six guys to sign up, and we put together a good card for the event which took place on November 21, 1997. Bruce slipped in two or three other fights to make it a full evening.

I was matched up with Bill Logan, who was a bearded writer. I never knew much about Bill, except that he was about my size and weight, and a few years younger. He was a game fighter and we had a good match. Bill Hunnicutt and I put together a great entourage of people to come and watch us. Bill Hunnicutt fought a young Wall Street guy who tried to take his head off in the first or second round. I was actually worried about Bill for a couple minutes, as he was backed up against the ropes against a fury of punches. But then I saw his opponent begin to tire and Bill start to take control. By the third round, Bill proved he was the stronger fighter, and coasted to a very strong finish. Had I been judging the fight, I would have given it to Bill hands down. After the fights, we each had rented a huge limousine, and took all of our friends to dinner in Little Italy, where we had a private room. It was a great way to celebrate the fantastic experience of having actually fought at Gleason's Gym. A new era had begun for me and my boxing career.

For some reason, I did not get down to Gleason's to participate in another one of their shows until June 11, 1999, when I was matched with a very good fighter, Craig Toomen, an architect. Bill Hunnicutt was also fighting that night, so we had planned a grand evening, complete with limos at the end of the fight and a big dinner in Little Italy.

Although this was his first white collar sparring night, Craig Toomen was no stranger to Gleason's. He was a regular there and a friend of Bruce Silverglade's. He was in great shape and a good boxer. He showed up that night wearing white gloves and white headgear. He had dark brown hair fashioned in a long ponytail, and cut quite a figure in the boxing ring— a boxer's version of "Darth Vader" from the movie *Star Wars*. Our first round was pretty even. In the second round, I landed two very good shots on him, which sobered him up. I could tell he came out in the third round to get even. He was throwing at me with everything he had, and he had a lot! He hit me with one good shot, but I got through the round okay.

However, I was glad when it was over. Again, this was a Gleason's white collar sparring match, so there was no formal winner or loser, and both Craig and I received a trophy for our efforts.

When I went to the corner, I was aware that there was something dripping from my lip. I looked down, and it was blood—my blood! My lip had been cut very badly during the fight. I am still not sure how it happened. I had taken many hard shots in my day, but never had a cut lip. The blood was really flowing, and apparently my lip had been cut very severely, as if with a knife. Normally, fighters are supposed to wrap the laces on their gloves, because the hard tips on the end of the lace can cut a fighter's face. Perhaps Craig had forgotten to

Colonel Alfred Richardson Simson

*John Oden, right, spars with Craig Toomen, left, at Gleason's
"White Collar Sparring Night" on June 11, 1999.*

wrap his laces and this was the reason, I don't know. Perhaps he just hit me hard enough to cut me—I'll *never* know. This cut did not affect the outcome of the fight, and I doubt if anyone in the audience even knew it. But did my lip ever bleed!

I went to the locker room after the fight. My lip was flowing like a river. Bob Jackson, a very experienced trainer who had managed many professional fighters, came in to help and put some salt on my lip. Although it was just a cut lip, I was tense and frustrated, as I had an entire entourage waiting for me outside, and I felt my shirt beginning to get wet, as I began perspiring while sitting there in the locker room. Bill Hunnicutt came in to see what was going on. I asked him to explain to everyone that I would get there as soon as I could, and he went out to appease the crowd. Bob Jackson kept working on my lip; the bleeding was beginning to slow down a little. People told me to go get stitches, but I said, "I've got friends ready to go to dinner."

Throughout this entire experience, there was one person constantly by my side. Chris Angle sat there, cool as a cucumber, doing what he could to calm me down and help wherever he could. I'll never forget it. Although a cut lip may not seem very serious, this was actually the worst injury I ever received in boxing, and in its own way, the experience was quite traumatic. I was so grateful to have Chris's steady, unwavering hand in my corner. His actions that night were representative of the remarkable camaraderie that I have come to love in the world of boxing.

This experience with my lip reminded me how lucky I had been with the lack of injuries I had received. I would have to attribute this to the excellent supervision these white collar boxing matches receive. At the first sign of trouble, the referees step right in and stop the fight. They disguise much of this by pretending to adjust headgear, put more tape on the glove, and so on. But what they are doing is really protecting the fighter from injury by giving him time to recover if he has been hit. This is true of supervised sparring as well. Bruce Silverglade has not had any serious injuries at Gleason's in his over 20 years of involvement.

I finally walked out of Gleason's bandaged, holding a towel to my face. My lip looked like it had been in a meat grinder,

Bill Hunnicutt, second from left, John Oden, third from right, and Chris Angle, far right, celebrate a successful night of boxing.

but I managed to get to the restaurant and co-host the dinner with Bill. When I got there, I found out that one of my artist friends, Colonel Alfred Richardson Simson, who had attended the fight with his lovely opera-singer wife, Veronica, had made a pencil drawing of my fight that night. It is a great drawing, and is proudly displayed amongst my boxing memorabilia in my apartment.

My lip healed quickly, and I was back in action in the NYAC boxing room the following week. The rest of the year passed rather uneventfully, and in early 2000, the NYAC announced that it would hold a Boxing Club Championship on May 11, 2000. This event was for the NYAC Boxing Club only, and not open to outsiders. I knew I had to enter this—I just wasn't sure whom I was going to fight. There were a few heavyweights around, including my friend, Bill Hunnicutt. Our head coaches, Dan O'Leary and Mike Fullam, made the matches, and Bill was matched with a good young heavyweight by the name of John McErlean, a first time fighter but a strong one. I knew Bill would have his hands full. I was also matched with a newcomer to the NYAC, Mark Settembre. Without question, Mark Settembre had the most awesome physical appearance of anyone with whom I had ever been matched. He was in great shape, and had an incredible build with big muscular arms. Anyone looking at Mark next to me would definitely bet on Mark winning the fight. He was very strong, but inexperienced, and had never been in a big fight. First-time fighters can be particularly dangerous, as they are often very nervous and attack with reckless abandon from the opening bell. Needless to say, I trained hard.

I employed an outside coach, Ron Johnson, so that I could have all the attention I wanted, and not detract from the other NYAC boxers who needed the time of our coaching staff. I was also becoming very friendly with Pete and Nick Spanakos, the amateur champions from the 1960s, who had taken a real interest in me. That evening my trainer, Ron

Johnson, was joined in my corner by Pete Spanakos. It proved to be a good combination.

My fight with Mark Settembre was scheduled to be the last fight of the evening. It was not billed as the main event, as the entire card that night was outstanding. Our fight just came last, as the heavyweights were usually last on the program. In fact, also in the heavyweight division that night just before my fight, Bill Hunnicutt won a hard-fought, close bout against John McErlean. I began my walk to the ring in the sixth floor gymnasium of the NYAC. It is a huge room. It was a big crowd, probably 300 to 400 people or more. Just being in the ring for an event like this was a somewhat daunting experience. These were the Club Championships! I climbed in the ring, and was introduced. Mark was wearing an all-black outfit, with a sleeveless shirt that showed off his muscular arms. My friends told me later that when they saw him, they truly feared for me—something I've heard on other occasions, as well.

Off we went. Mark had some trouble with his footing, and while swinging at me in the first round, actually fell down. This unsettled him. Later in the round, when he was coming in at me, I shoved him back, and he almost fell down again. I could tell he was shaken by these two slips.

Things settled down in rounds two and three, and we had a good bout. Pete Spanakos was whispering in my ear the entire time that I had easily won the fight. But then it was the judges' turn. Sure enough, I got the decision. What a triumphant moment for me! While I was not crowned heavyweight champion, and there are better heavyweights at the NYAC than me, I am the only heavyweight to have participated in both of the two Club Championships in the past decade, and won a heavyweight division fight both times. That does not qualify me for a title, but it does demand some respect. That and 75 cents will get me a cup of coffee from a street wagon in New York, but I nevertheless know I achieved something that night. I felt proud.

Below is an article from *The Winged Foot* of July 2000, describing my fight:

> *Finally, in the matchup that everyone had been wait-*
> *ing for, "The Pecos Kid," John Oden, stepped into the*
> *ring against burly Mark Settembre. Although Settembre*
> *appeared to be the better conditioned athlete, once again*
> *skill and experience proved to be the decisive factor.*
> *Oden, another veteran of the NYAC boxing stable, was*
> *the only returning competitor from the previous decade's*
> *Championships. Like the Hurricane before him, John*
> *was able to keep his opponent at bay with his tenacious*
> *left jab that stopped Mark cold every time it looked as*
> *though he was getting started. Although Settembre put on*
> *a gallant effort, the Pecos Kid was too quick for his more*
> *muscular foe.*

In the meantime, in the early summer of 2000, Bruce Silverglade was putting together a group to go to London to fight a team from The Real Fight Club in London, England. I was thinking about doing this, and needed to stay in shape. I participated in the next two white collar sparring nights at Gleason's Gym. I thought Mark Settembre might enjoy fighting at Gleason's, as well as appreciate the opportunity to get some experience under his belt, so I invited him to go down to Gleason's with me to be my opponent for a white collar sparring night to be held on June 2, 2000.

This time he was ready for me. He put on a much better exhibition this time, and we had a very tough fight. He hit me with a really hard head shot, and my neck was stiff for days. Again, as in all Gleason's white collar bouts, it was a non-decision fight. But it got me ready for London, and I knew it was unlikely I would have a tougher opponent than Mark Settembre.

Through this, Gleason's Gym and I were becoming good friends. I enjoyed working out there on Saturday mornings, in particular. There were so many different people available to spar with, all shapes and sizes—no two were alike. I was becoming very friendly with many of the regulars; the pros often showed up, too. One morning that year, I remember marveling at a really big man who moved like a ballet dancer but hit like a wrecking ball. Some of the men had necks like fire hydrants, backs like anvils, and legs like tree trunks. Yet their movements in the ring had a speed, grace, and ease that defied logic.

I work closely with my trainer to pick my sparring partners. Certainly, not everyone who goes to Gleason's would automatically qualify to be my opponent. While I am always seeking to challenge myself, boxing is no place for illusions, and it could actually be dangerous for me to kid myself into thinking I am better than I am or build up a false sense of security. I know well there are boxers at Gleason's who could dispatch me within seconds of the opening bell. I know that the controlled white collar sparring I do is nothing like the threatening dance that is high stakes professional boxing. Yet, I am very comfortable there, and get a good workout every time I make the trip.

Up until this point, I had had a pretty good run at the NYAC, and at Gleason's white collar sparring nights. I had received some really good press coverage. I had become known as a boxer, and many of my friends and clients were intrigued by that. I liked the image of being a boxer and I enjoyed the publicity. After all, it was harmless and actually made me feel like a more interesting person. So was I ready for my next challenge? Was I ready to fight in London? Was I ready to journey to the country where the term sweet science was born?

CHAPTER

7

LONDON CALLING

When a man is tired of London, he is tired of life.
—SAMUEL JOHNSON, ENGLISH POET

In the year 2000, Alan Lacey, a promoter in London with a passion for boxing, recruited a British team to take on the Americans in their own backyard—in Gleason's Gym. Alan Lacey and Bruce Silverglade arranged for this white collar sparring night on May 2, 2000, between the London "team"—anyone who answered the ad and met with Alan's approval—and a team from Gleason's selected by Bruce. The evening at Gleason's was a great success, with over 10 bouts on the card, and a white collar rivalry between the United States and London was born. These bouts were fought in the true white collar sparring style, with no winner or loser declared, and both participants receiving a trophy.

According to Stephen Moss, a writer for *The Guardian* in London, "One reason for the new-found interest in boxing in the United Kingdom was the film *Fight Club,* which had come out a few months earlier. Its premise is that life is dull and ritualized, that we have lost our spirit and freedom, that society is a machine which enmeshes us. Its message—take control. Gleason's Gym had anticipated *Fight Club* by more than a decade, attracting men, and eventually, women, who want to exercise and, perhaps to exorcise some personal demon. 'Many people who come here are trying to prove something to themselves,' says Bruce Silverglade. 'Many of them have an agenda.'"

England has a great tradition of boxing, and has played an enormous role in bringing the sport forward in its development. The English spirit is rugged, athletic, and tough. For example, one of the true national sports of the English is rugby, a difficult and very physical game. For this reason, boxing has flourished there for centuries, and continues strong today. Lennox Lewis, the recently retired Heavyweight Boxing Champion of the World, calls London home. Many world and amateur boxing champions have had roots there. The country also has a long history of club fighting and backroom fighting at the amateur level.

I attended the May 2, 2000 event which pitted London against New York. To me, the aspect of international competition, even at the white collar level, made the sport even more interesting. It was an amazing night with many good white collar bouts. My former opponent, Craig Toomen, knocked down the big British heavyweight, Craig Ashcroft, in the first round and looked extremely impressive. I also saw the British promoter, Alan Lacey, fight one of the bouts that evening, and he moved quite well in the ring. Alan is a distinguished looking man who looks like an English version of an aging and graying General George Armstrong Custer. He sports a goatee and wears double-breasted suits. Alan Lacey was in the business of travel promotion prior to setting up The Real Fight Club in 2001. He always had the boxing "bug," and even tried his hand with the promotion of one professional boxer prior to his entry into white collar boxing.

Even more important at those fights on May 2, 2000, was the talk of bouts scheduled in London for July between a

Gleason's team organized by Bruce Silverglade and a London team by Alan Lacey. Bruce told me he wanted to put me on the Gleason's team. I accepted his invitation, and began training in dead earnest.

About that time, I decided to switch trainers. I had used professional trainers away from the NYAC trainers for some time, as I wanted as much attention as possible and found that I could accomplish that best by hiring my own trainer and letting the younger members of the NYAC Boxing Team share the two or three trainers the team had at that time. I had observed a very good trainer named Ricky Young, who was head of the Columbia University Boxing Team. Ricky was a former pro, with a record of 18–4. His photograph from his days as a professional boxer hangs on the wall of Gleason's Gym. He is an excellent trainer, and a terrific human being. In addition to his duties at Columbia, he is a motivational speaker. He also organizes motivational conferences, featuring speakers such as Deepak Chopra. In fact, Ricky lured Chopra for his first speaking engagement in Harlem. Ricky and I began working out regularly, including a trip to Gleason's every Saturday morning, in anticipation of going to London to fight in July.

In June, I learned that the London event was to be called Capital Punishment, as it pitted Wall Street professionals in New York versus Threadneedle Street (the financial district of London) professionals in London. It was to be held at the Broadgate Arena, an open air theater in the middle of the financial district. More than 3,000 people would attend the event, which was to occur at the end of the business day on Thursday, July 13, 2000. In addition, a documentary movie of the event would be made.

Things were going well for me in my boxing career, and I was training hard and enjoying the sport. Then tragedy struck. When I took up boxing in 1992, I had also taken up one other sport—basketball. My focus had always been on boxing, but I also enjoyed basketball, and used it for cross-training purposes.

Exactly four weeks before the fight, on June 16, 2000, I was playing basketball with my Friday morning basketball group. I leaped high in the air for a rebound, got it, and came down hard. I landed on my left foot, which did not hold, and I came crashing to the ground. The result was one of the loudest "pops" I have ever heard a bone make. The whole gym heard it. Activity stopped all around me. I knew I had done something bad. The first thing I thought of was my upcoming trip to London to fight in Capital Punishment.

I took my shoe off and applied ice. My foot immediately began to swell and started hurting. I limped off the court, and headed for home, which was one block away. From there I went to the doctor who x-rayed the foot and announced that I had a cracked fibula, the bone above the ankle. He held out very little hope that I would make the trip to London to fight in July.

But I wasn't giving up that easily. I asked the doctor what the best course of action would be to increase my chances of being able to go. He put me on crutches and in a walking cast, and told me that I should begin immediate physical therapy. I went to a special therapist who works with professional athletes. With him, I developed a twice-a-day exercise regimen which I adhered to religiously, despite my many professional commitments. My doctor looked at the foot once or twice a week, and commented that I seemed to be making progress. In about two weeks, he gave me a soft cast, and I began light sparring. It made me very nervous to spar, as I could feel the vulnerability of my fibula and the entire area around my ankle. Even with the soft cast, I took it very easy. Meanwhile, I was not able to run, lift weights, and do the things I normally do. Putting any kind of pressure on the foot resulted in a great deal of pain.

The week prior to the trip to London, I stepped up my workouts and my sparring. I was determined to make the trip and fight. I was scheduled to leave on Monday for the fight on

Thursday, July 13, 2000. My doctor somewhat reluctantly cleared me to go on Friday, July 8. I was thrilled, but nervous about my foot and ankle. I was determined to do this, because I knew it would be the chance of a lifetime. I learned that I was to fight Dr. Marcus Overhaus, a 30-something-year-old derivatives trader at Deutsche Bank AG in London. I was interviewed by the press in London on Tuesday before the fights, and learned that one of the London team members had been widely quoted as saying that he wanted to knock his opponent out. After the fight, I discovered that this was Dr. Overhaus.

Thursday arrived, and I went to the designated meeting place at the requested 3 P.M. for the weigh-in. All of the fighters were assembled. I was using my crutches and the walking cast, as per my doctor's instructions. Heads turned as I walked up—I guess not too many fighters come to fight sporting crutches and a walking cast. There was a lot of publicity surrounding the event. I had been quoted in the Sunday papers in London, and there were TV cameras at our weigh-in. It was extremely exciting.

Finally, the event began. It had rained on and off since I had been in London, but cleared up just in time for the show, which was great since we were in an outdoor arena. We were the third fight. Apparently, Dr. Overhaus was an important guy at Deutsche Bank, as he had 250 people at ringside. Off we went. Our fight was refereed by Adrian Dodson, former Super Middleweight Champion of the world and currently seeking to regain the title. Adrian is a very knowledgeable boxing person, a professional boxer originally from New York who cut his teeth in boxing at Gleason's and now resides in London. He was in complete control of the fight at all times, which is always comforting to a fighter. My strategy was to move around as much as I could and avoid tough exchanges and getting hit, as this might further injure my ankle. I intended to get just enough good shots in to let my opponent and the audience know that I had come to fight, but not try to engage in any more tough exchanges and close contact than necessary, to keep my ankle out of harm's way. This strategy worked well in the first round. In the second round, Dr. Overhaus came at me full force, and I let him have it. I hit him so hard I thought I was going to knock him down. By doing so, I gained his respect, and had no problems with him the rest of the fight. However, because my training had been curtailed due to my injury, I found myself tiring in the third round. I was very glad to hear the final bell ring.

It seemed to me that the London guys, as a whole, came out ahead of our guys that night. There were some pretty tough fights, and the color of red was seen during several of the bouts, as there were many bloody noses, cuts, and other injuries. There were 12 to 14 fights, and because we had only brought about nine fighters, some of the fights were Brits versus Brits. Regardless, it was a great night and a terrific experience. I was truly glad I'd made the extra effort to train and go. My ankle was still tender, but had come out fine. It now had plenty of time to heal, and I accomplished what many had thought to be impossible when the injury to the fibula in my ankle first occurred.

I made several friends on the London team during the Capital Punishment bouts. One was a chap by the name of Richard Williams, who received a lot of press coverage since he was a well-known intellectual in London, an Oxford graduate in languages with a doctorate in history from London University. He is a librarian by training, currently working at the London & Quandrant Housing Trust. He and I had received as much pre-fight press coverage as anyone before the fight, so we had sought out each other and spent some time together after the fights. We then corresponded in the days following the fights, and still do. In short, we developed a friendship.

Some time in the late summer of 2000, Bruce Silverglade announced that the London fighters would be traveling to

New York in November. I volunteered to fight for the Gleason's team. As the date got closer, Bruce told me I was going to be matched with my new friend, Richard Williams. I didn't mind this, as I frequently do not know who I am to be matched with prior to a fight, and I thought that Richard would be an interesting opponent. I had already told him that he could stay in my spare bedroom for the trip, before I knew that he and I would fight. I honored that commitment, and Richard arrived on a Monday night for the week. The fights were on Friday, November 17.

Also in town for this event was my friend, Jack Kendrick, from Sweden, where he lived. He was also staying in my apartment, as he often did when he came into town. I introduced him to Richard Williams, and the bonding was almost instantaneous. Besides sharing a love for boxing, the three of us all enjoy athletics, as well as the study of history, poetry, and literature. We shared a good meal together the night before the fight. I made the New York Athletic Club available to Richard for his daily workouts.

The night of the big fights arrived, and I had a sizable entourage in my corner. Richard, Jack, and I rode down together. Jack was to be my corner man, along with Pete Spanakos. I always like to be the third fight at Gleason's, as it does not have the pressure and anticipation of being the first fight. By the time the third fight rolls around, the audience is a little loosened up and things are usually flowing pretty smoothly. Yet, everyone is still very attentive to what is going on in the ring. Also, by going on third, there is plenty of time to shower and change into street clothes and catch a few of the fights at the end of the show. Then I am ready to go "out on the town" the moment the fights are over. Thus, the third fight was our position on the card. I think the third fight is the "sweet spot" on a white collar (noncompetitive) boxing card.

By this time Richard had become a true friend, and I felt a little odd about fighting him, particularly since he was staying in my apartment. But when the call came for "seconds out," and the bell rang to begin the fight, we both went about our business. Richard rushed me early, and I stood firm and hit back hard. To my amazement, he crumpled to the canvas. I realized I was stronger than he, and finished the other two rounds displaying good boxing skill, but not trying to take his head off. We had a good bout. Nick Spanakos, who was Muhammad Ali's roommate on the 1960 Olympic team in Rome, summarized it thusly in a press release he wrote the following day:

> The main event featured my friend John Oden, a tall, silver haired monetary heavy hitter from the prestigious Wall Street firm, Bernstein, by day, and a titular prizefighter by night with a couple of heavyweight titles from the NYAC (New York Athletic Club) and a string of winning bouts, battling against a studious, quiet, balding Brit, Richard Williams, a librarian. Covering this epic international contest amongst these titans was a television crew flown over from England. John scored with snappy left jabs and pain killing right hands. The brave Brit went down for the count in the first round. The next two rounds the American pummeled his opponent but executed it minus the rage, and thirst for blood that ordinary boxers do to satisfy the fight fans so they can exalt in this socially accepted violence. I hope this compassionate type of battle does not diminish from the mythic, and mystic, glow of the warrior-boxer that has enthralled the pugilistic world for centuries.

This was admittedly written by a good friend, and I am aware (and appreciative) of its bias. For his part, Richard Williams did a fine job, and we had a great night. Shortly thereafter we were all loaded into the limo I had contracted for the evening, and off we went for a fabulous evening in Little Italy.

So, in the year 2000, the Gleason's team under Bruce Silverglade had three encounters with Alan Lacey's British boxers: at Gleason's in May, Capital Punishment in London in July, and at Gleason's in November. By any counts, this was a great first year. And I fought in two out of three of them. Following these three fights, Alan Lacey founded The Real Fight Club in 2001, a white collar boxing promotion company based in London (Alan's matches have no relation to the barbarism projected in the film *Fight Club*), which regularly has white collar sparring matches with huge crowds in large hotel venues in London, many of them black tie fundraisers. The attraction, according to Lacey is, "Death or glory. Boxing is a chance to make their schoolboy fantasies come true."

I should probably comment on the movie *Fight Club*, which had both violent and unrealistic elements. The movie depicted bored office workers who amuse themselves in their free time by beating up each other with brutal, bare-knuckle boxing matches set in a clandestine, club-like, underground backdrop. Their beaten and battered faces served as a red badge of courage to those co-workers and friends who were privileged to know about the secret, anarchic subculture they call "Fight Club." Their leader, the character played by Brad Pitt, becomes somewhat of a cult hero, and the members spiral downward in self-destruction and escape from normalcy. This is in sharp contrast to Alan Lacey's The Real Fight Club, which is an above-board, above-ground, successful organization of British professionals who box for exercise, competition and fun, in a gloved, fully supervised, white collar boxing setting. Though a comparison can be made to both groups participating in the unique sport of boxing, the manner and context in which the two groups approach the sport are very different, and defy any meaningful comparison. Further discussion involving the words "fight club" will confine itself to Alan Lacey's The Real Fight Club, only.

When Alan established The Real Fight Club, he set forth four rules of the club:

"Rule #1—Fight for Love not Money
Rule #2—Come from the City not the Streets
Rule #3—Enjoy the buzz
Rule #4—You don't agree with it? Don't watch!"

I am not sure if The Real Fight Club still has these rules, but I could definitely relate to them. For Rule #1, I am not fighting for the money; I have a good job which more than pays the rent. I love the sport. For Rule #2, I am a Wall Street professional. Even though I have humble, small-town beginnings, I had a good solid upbringing by great parents, who were constantly with me in my formative years. I was not raised in a "project" or an orphanage. I have a good education and a good job. Regarding Rule #3, I love the crowds and the hype surrounding a fight, even at the white collar level. I have enjoyed the publicity I have received. And, as far as Rule #4 goes, I actually think that if more people watched and gave it a chance, they would understand and appreciate it more. Despite this rule, I encourage people to come and watch. So, in summary, as far as these rules go, I would only take issue somewhat with Rule #4. The others are right on.

In the spring of 2001, Bruce Silverglade announced another fight in London, which was to be held on June 14, in London. He was looking for volunteers for the Gleason's team, and I could not resist. I started training very hard for the trip, pleased that this time I did not have to worry about my foot. It was a good thing I did. A few days before the fight, I learned that I was to fight Lee Victory, a bond trader with Cantor Fitzgerald. I had spoken to Alan Lacey "across the pond" a few days before the fight, and he told me he thought Lee would be a good match for me. He was younger (37), shorter (5'9"), and lighter (190 pounds) than me. Alan told me that he had sparred with Lee, and thought I should use my jab to keep him away and I would be fine. This all sounded fine to me, as I was quite accustomed to younger opponents, and my jab was my most reliable weapon.

I had been training with both Jack Kendrick and Ricky Young for this fight, as it was an important one for me. I trained as hard as I have ever trained for a fight, and really concentrated on getting in shape. Neither Jack nor Ricky could attend this fight in London, so my corner was going to be empty, except for someone from Gleason's who I had probably not worked with before. Jack sensed this, and prior to my leaving, placed the following note in my hands:

John,

Although the human condition is complex, it is still simple, and you must carry this idea with you to your London fight—that is, for all the things that will be going on in your mind, before and during the fight, you must not give in to the complexities, rather keep them in a shell of simplicity. He is 5′9″ and you can dominate him with your left jab (through the head, not to the head) and then, when the opportunity comes, then drop your big right hand down the pike. Be moderate in your footwork but kick it up a gear when needed. Don't lift the leg when you are crowded, and never let him hear a sound from you if he bangs you to the body. Push off, when crowded, rather than staying inside with clinches. Don't forget to just hold him off by laying your open glove on his eyes and forehead. But mostly, John, realize your improvement and your strengths by believing them! No trainer can instill that in you—only you can do it. You have been to the well against all kinds of styles, and you have achieved victories, not defeats. Believe, believe in yourself. I'll be with you in spirit, therefore I'll be with

you! It's another hill for you, and the view will be won-
derful. You are privileged to be competing, so honor that
privilege by your talent, your courage, your humility, and
your compassion, and along with God's blessing and the
ghosts of your kin, you will.

Jack Kendrick

Needless to say, I was extremely touched by these
thoughts, and carried them with me every step of the way to
London and into the ring with me that night. I saw Lee
Victory in the locker room shortly before the fight. He was
very serious looking, a sort of somber Mr. Clean, in that he
was on the stockier side, and had a bald head—he had shaved
his head for the fight, I believe. He shook my hand in the
locker room, as the two team's locker rooms were right next
to each other, but was extremely serious. I could tell he was
going to be trouble.

The event was a black tie fundraiser for charity in the
Royal National Hotel in Russell Square. The evening was a
long one, starting with cocktails at 7 P.M., dinner at 8 P.M., and
the fights scheduled to begin at 9:30 P.M. There was an exhibition of some sort at the beginning, and then Lee and I were
the first fight. By the time we arrived in the ring, the crowd
was loaded for bear. They had been drinking since
7 P.M., and were having a great time. The room was buzzing
with electricity, excitement, and alcohol. This time, instead of
the excellent refereeing of Adrian Dodson that I enjoyed in
my previous London bout, our bout was to be refereed by a
chap who seemed to have limited boxing knowledge. This
proved to be a distraction, and is very atypical of Alan's other
referees I have observed, who have been terrific. I am confident it was an isolated case, and not likely to be repeated.

Lee Victory may be the single toughest opponent of my
career. He came at me from the opening bell. I could tell I was

going to have to give it my all just to survive this fight. He landed a couple of good shots, and I knew it was now or never. I hit him with everything I had, once, then again. A lesser man would have gone down. I really rocked him. He was rattled, but stayed on his feet. I took my share of punishment from him. The round ended. Round two was more of the same. His attacks were so vicious and he came straight at me, coming in low to my body because he was smaller than me. I would occasionally tie him up, meaning I would clinch with him when he came in close rather than engage in a lot of inside or close quarter fighting, as a form of self defense. As my jab is my best weapon, and because of my long arms, I like to keep people at a distance and score points by using it. Lee Victory kept charging me, trying to come inside, and I would just tie him up, rather than go toe to toe with him at close range. This is a perfectly acceptable thing to do. However, the referee did not know this and criticized me for doing so. I almost felt like punching him out, he was such a distraction. The second round ended and I was exhausted.

I looked over at Bruce Silverglade, and I am sure he could tell how exhausted I was. I was relieved to know that Bruce was on the bell, as I knew he would ring it early if I really got in trouble—I had seen him do that before to protect boxers from getting hurt. I got through the third round somehow, and was never more glad to hear the final bell ring. I did not feel as though I experienced the sweet science that day. I feel that my survival instincts took over, and my training and mental preparation was overcome by instinctive fears to protect myself. I did not perform at my best level, even though it turned out to be a pretty good fight. I regret I did not keep my composure and fight up to my potential that evening.

Before the fight, I had promised Richard Quest, a famous announcer with CNN in London, that I would do a post-fight interview. I was so exhausted that I forgot I'd made this promise. I watched the next fight, and then went quietly to the dressing room to shower and change. I am well familiar with the old cliché "you know it is a bad day when there's a crew from *60 Minutes* in your company's lobby." Well, when I got to the dressing room, exhausted and hurting in several places, there was Richard Quest and a camera crew from CNN. The interview ended up being a good one, and was shown all over the world. I got calls from friends of mine that I had not heard from in years, who said how impressed they were with what I'd said. The fight clips were apparently good, as well.

Almost three months later to the day, the infamous September 11 attacks on the World Trade Center in New York City occurred. One of the firms hit hardest was Cantor Fitzgerald. I placed a call on that day, September 11, to Lee Victory, who worked for Cantor Fitzgerald in London, to make sure he was okay, and express my sympathy for his colleagues who had not been so fortunate. I think he appreciated the call, and when I saw him the next year in London, he was very friendly to me. Despite the hard fight which Lee and I had, we had respect for each other and developed a friendship after the fight.

In March of the following year, I accompanied the Gleason's team to another black tie fundraiser in London, this time to raise funds for the families of the victims of September 11. My brother, Bill Oden, had just died an untimely death of cancer the month before, and I was in no condition to fight. My brother was a very outdoors person, a builder and a contractor, who stayed in the sun all day long. He was 20 years older than me, and contracted the deadly cancer melanoma. Unfortunately, when it was diagnosed, it was in its advanced stages. I had told Bruce I would participate when the bouts were announced in December, only to find out a few days later of my brother's serious condition. I made two trips to Pecos to see him before he died in mid-February of 2002. Along the way, I told Alan Lacey and Bruce Silverglade that it was unlikely I would be able to fulfill my commitment to participate in the March bouts in London.

However, I had a lot of fun as a spectator and the bond between the British and Gleason's teams was growing even stronger. When I go to Gleason's or the New York Athletic Club as a spectator, I really enjoy it, because I usually know many of the people fighting. Sometimes at Gleason's, Bruce Silverglade introduces me to the audience. Alan Lacey has made the same offer to me in London on occasion. On more than one event at the New York Athletic Club, I have been asked to be the master of ceremonies for the evening. I also try to be helpful to those I know who are fighting as the evening progresses. It is because I have "earned my spurs" as a fighter that I can enjoy myself so much as a spectator—it just gives me a different perspective on the evening's activities. This unique perspective, which I feel I have earned, makes everything even more fun.

The Real Fight Club has really grown and prospered, and had become the main white collar boxing promotion company in London. According to Adrian Dodson, with whom I've since become good friends, "White collar boxing is now bigger in the United Kingdom than professional boxing." Adrian was born in New York, and cut his teeth boxing at Gleason's. He now resides in London, where he trains and lives with his family.

In the past four years, almost 4,000 lawyers, bankers, judges and other "suits"—mostly men in their twenties, thirties, and forties, have joined London's The Real Fight Club, which is growing rapidly. According to Alan, white collar boxing is the fastest growing sport in the United Kingdom, and the only real growth area in the boxing business there. In the beginning, Lacey says he got maybe one new member a month. Now he claims six a day from all over Britain. Much of this transformation in the United Kingdom boxing took place in just a few years, since Alan Lacey made his journey to Gleason's in May of 2000. He feels it is positioned to grow exponentially over the next few years. To join The Real Fight Club, men (there are still only a handful of women boxers in London) undergo a physical examination and pay £140, which doesn't include any of the training sessions (which cost from £14). The fights have grown from occasional to nearly every month, and are held at two kinds of venues: places like York Hall, which attracts serious fight fans, and plush London hotels, which attract the dinner-jacket crowd and a portion of the proceeds go to charity. Since its inception, The Real Fight Club has hosted 41 boxing shows, as of April 2005. In addition, according to Alan, "the media interest is completely out of balance with the size of the operation—there is huge interest from the media in white collar boxing." The website of The Real Fight Club is www.therealfightclub.co.uk.

The Real Fight Club has a rival in Australia—the Australian Academy of Boxing—which offers white collar boxing training and competitions. The sport is also starting in Singapore, where the U2 Can Gym, a converted chicken shed, recently bought a boxing ring and has begin to offer serious training. Among the instructors: an ex-head boxing coach for the Singapore Army. Alan Lacey has interest in making matches from people and clubs all over the world, including places like Germany, South Africa, Russia, Canada, Dubai, Hong Kong, and Shanghai, to mention just a few.

In 2002, Alan Lacey honored me by asking me to be on the Board of Directors of the newly formed International White Collar Boxing Association. Alan intends for this organization to be the governing board for white collar boxing around the world. He is assembling an excellent group of white collar boxers, mostly British boxers, including my friend, Richard Williams. I look forward to serving on this board and advancing the efforts of white collar boxing and the sweet science around the world.

CHAPTER 8

IN THE SPOTLIGHT

There is no such thing as bad publicity.
—ANONYMOUS

I've always been something of a publicity hound. Even in high school, I enjoyed getting my name in the school newspaper. I was from a small town, and there wasn't too much to talk about in the newspaper but people and what they were doing.

Getting your name in the New York newspapers is a whole different ballgame. There are a lot of extremely wealthy, powerful people in this city. If you're not Mayor Bloomberg or Donald Trump, you need to do something quite extraordinary to get meaningful press coverage. When I was in the real estate business, I was quoted a lot in the industry rag, *Commercial Property News*. At Bernstein, the company does not encourage a lot of interviews with the media, unless you are on the research side of the firm, which I am not. Then I started boxing.

Boxing gets both good and bad publicity. At the end of the day, I think that the public absolutely loves a major, professional, big-time boxing match. Major celebrities turn out for the really big matches in Las Vegas, Atlantic City, Madison Square Garden, and other venues. A championship boxing match commands media attention like no other sport. However, at times the sport suffers from participants who do not conduct themselves in a sportsmanlike manner either in or out of the ring.

In recent years, white collar boxing has had its share of attention, as the public has focused more than ever on health and physical fitness. The lion's share of the attention, at least in this country, has gone to Gleason's Gym and Bruce Silverglade. White collar boxing has been the subject of numerous newspaper and magazine articles, even television documentaries, and Bruce has become its de facto spokesperson. As he fields these requests, he introduces his boxers to the press when it's appropriate for the subject matter being written about. Because there is a lot of favorable publicity surrounding the intersection of the Wall Street community with the boxing community and because I am a legitimate Wall Street professional, I'm often called upon to be interviewed for a story. The general public, it seems, is fascinated by Wall Street professionals who box.

Because of this, I have been the subject of many stories. I have had articles published in many of the major newspapers in New York City and around the country, as well as several national magazines, regarding my career as a white collar boxer. I have enjoyed this, and feel that it does not hurt me professionally or personally. An English film company made a documentary film about white collar boxing, and included footage from the white collar boxing event in London termed Capital Punishment on July 13, 2000, in which part of my fight appeared.

In September of 2000, *Trader's Magazine*, a publication read by traders in the financial markets and exchanges, did a feature article on amateur boxing, in which I was extensively quoted and photographed. My firm reproduced the article so I could distribute it to clients. It came out very well, and my company was obviously not displeased. If I'd hired a PR agency, I could not have created a more impressive and unique package for myself and my business.

One day in 2001, I was walking up Madison Avenue, and came upon the Margo Feiden Galleries. Margo Feiden is the exclusive representative of the art of the famous caricaturist, Al Hirschfeld. Mr. Hirschfeld passed away in 2003 at the ripe old age of 99, and had been drawing show business and other personalities all of his life. While he had drawn actors and even one U.S. President (Reagan) in a boxing ring, it appears that the only *real* boxer Mr. Hirschfeld had drawn was the great Muhammad Ali. I went to the gallery, met Margo Feiden, and the wheels began to turn in my head. After some discussion, we agreed that Mr. Hirschfeld would make me his next subject, in full boxing attire. I actually posed for him in his townhouse in Manhattan. I must have been one of his last subjects, as he passed away a few months after my work was completed. The end result was nothing less than remarkable, and is proudly displayed in my home. With Margo Feiden's permission, I had 6" x 9" folded cards made up of this drawing, which I use all the time to send notes to friends and clients.

Then came my big break. MSNBC wanted to do a one-hour documentary film on white collar boxing, and my name was given to them by Bruce Silverglade at Gleason's. I fit the part, as they were looking for a successful Wall Street executive who boxed. Bruce also provided MSNBC with the names of two others: Phil Maier, who is a New York City judge, and Edwin Calderon, who works in investments at Teacher's Insurance. Over the course of several weeks, the producers came into my home, my office, the NYAC. They followed me out socially in the evening and to work in the morning. They accompanied me on my 5 A.M. run in Central Park. I felt like a real celebrity. They gave the same attention to Phil and Edwin.

All of this led up to a fight at Gleason's Gym one Friday night. It was originally scheduled for Friday, September 14, 2001. However, because of the terrorist attacks on the city on

September 11, the fight had to be postponed. The buildup to a fight is a very lengthy and hard process, requiring much training, discipline, and focus. I have never had a fight for which I trained hard either postponed or cancelled. This has happened to friends of mine, and I always empathized with them, knowing how difficult a task the mental and physical preparation for a fight can be. However, in the immediate aftermath of 9/11, my fight seemed trivial in relation to this turn of world events. The World Trade Center had been a fixture in my mind's eye for many, many years. One of my favorite training runs was to leave from Gleason's at sunrise and run across the Brooklyn Bridge and back, in full view of the World Trade Center both ways, as the sun was rising over New York City. I shall never forget those runs and that view. The beauty and tranquility were indescribable. Ironically, the film crew for MSNBC had originally planned to film my run over the Brooklyn Bridge on the morning of 9/11. It was only at the last minute on September 10 that they changed their mind, and we agreed to film a run in Central Park on September 12. I can just imagine what it might have been like to have stood on the Brooklyn Bridge that morning and to have watched that horrific scene.

I spent the days of aftermath of the World Trade Center collapse sequestered in my apartment writing about one of my favorite topics—the history of New York City. On occasion, I would go for a run in Central Park. These actions over those few days were very therapeutic. When I ventured out into the City during that period, it was a most surreal time, almost as if the world was in slow motion, and the people were actors in a play. I was content to deal with these events by my writing and my running. I felt helpless to do anything else.

The fights were eventually rescheduled to Friday, October 19, 2001. Despite the heaviness still hovering over New York City and rest of the world, a number of my friends attended the fights and the entire evening was great fun. I think those who attended were ready for some kind of break in the cloud that had fallen over everyone since 9/11. I fought a very tough guy by the name of Perry D'Alessio, who runs his own accounting firm. I had met Perry in London. He is in his mid-thirties, strong, and outweighed me by about 20 pounds. Our fight that night was nothing particularly special, and I do not feel either Perry or I tasted the sweet science. Nevertheless we had a good bout, which came off very well in front of the cameras. So I was pleased with a decent performance.

I had told my sparring partner at the NYAC, Chris Angle, about the fights, and he volunteered to fight Edwin Calderon, who is one of the most talented boxers at Gleason's. He and Edwin had a great bout. The fight of the night was Judge Phil Maier, who fought an auto mechanic from Texas. There was quite a buildup to this fight, as the auto mechanic had driven all the way from Texas, just to fight at Gleason's Gym. He was boasting to anyone who would listen before the fight that he intended to knock out Phil Maier. Phil has had about 50 white collar bouts, and is a very composed fighter and person. He took all this in stride.

The fight between Phil Maier and the guy from Texas (let's call him "Texas") started fast. Texas was obviously there to score a knockout, and he came out very strong. Phil was fighting defensively, but strategically. The cameras zoomed in on the fighters between rounds. Between rounds two and three, David Lawrence (Phil's trainer and one of the first white collar boxers) spoke very directly to Phil. He told Phil that Texas had been disrespectful to him, and that Phil should go ahead and knock him out because of all the boasting and negative things that Texas had said to and about Phil. I have known Phil for a long time, and have never known him to go for a knockout. Nevertheless, as I was warming up for my fight, which was only two fights away, I heard a loud yell from the crowd. I was then told that Phil Maier had knocked Texas out. It was a great moment, and was captured very well on the film.

David Lawrence, as I've mentioned before, had participated in the first Gleason's white collar sparring night; he was also the man I had read about in the *Time* article on the Wall Street Charity bouts back in 1986. During the making of this documentary, I learned several things about him. First, he had become obsessed with boxing, and actually turned pro. He had about six professional fights, all ending in knockouts—he knocked four guys out and was knocked out twice himself. Simultaneously, he had gotten some bad tax advice, which resulted in his having to spend time in prison. I have since gotten to know David Lawrence reasonably well, as he is a fixture at Gleason's. Though he is hardly a lord of Wall Street at this point in his career, on any objective basis, he is a unique guy. He is one of the regular trainers there, working 5-6 days a week. He takes his job seriously, and is a good trainer. He writes poetry, and is very well spoken (he has a Ph.D., as mentioned earlier). He is often filmed reading his poetry when people do documentary films about Gleason's. He's a lot of fun to be around. I have always been amazed at how circumstances can turn dramatically in a person's life, and it's interesting to see how various people react to the tumult. David Lawrence has traveled the winding road from highly paid Wall Street tycoon to boxing trainer and poet, and has made the ride in fine shape.

Following the fights on October 19, 2001, I had an enormous limo waiting, and took my entourage to a celebration dinner at a nearby Italian restaurant. There were about 20 of us, and we had a very festive evening, suitable for the tough fight I'd endured. I found out that my opponent, Perry D'Alessio, had coincidentally taken his supporters to the same restaurant. I went over to Perry's table and presented him with a bottle of wine. It was truly a great evening.

The result of all this was a one-hour documentary film, which was broadcast on MSNBC in October of 2002, entitled *Fight Night*. I could not miss this opportunity for a little "self-promotion." Besides, this was truly a fun moment for me. I engraved an invitation on the Hirschfeld cards to a live viewing of the show at my apartment. It read like this:

John E. Oden
Cordially Invites You to Be Present
For His TELEVISION DEBUT
And to join him
From 8:30–11:30 p.m. on Sunday, October 20, 2002
To view the Original Broadcast of *FIGHT NIGHT,*
a one-hour MSNBC television special starring
John E. Oden "The Pecos Kid"
(and other boxers from Gleason's Gym)
To be aired at 10 P.M.,
with special introductions at 9:45 P.M.
R.S.V.P Cocktails and Hors d' oeuvres
Dressy Casual

I invited many of my top clients, as well as some extremely influential people in New York City and around the country to this party. Inviting people to this event was a little like sending Christmas cards—I contacted lots of people who lived very far away, and whom I assumed could not come on short notice (I only had 10 days' notice myself). However, the invitation gave them notice of the show's airing, so they could watch it in their own homes that evening.

The response was truly amazing. Almost everyone I invited showed up. People did not know what to expect, but came both out of friendship to me and general curiosity.

The event itself could not have been better. Everyone who was in the film was there, including all of the fighters except Chris Angle (who had a flat tire and could not come), all of the boxing trainers (including David Lawrence), and Bruce Silverglade. My opponent, Perry D'Alessio, who has become a good friend, also attended. I made the most of it, playing music from the movie soundtrack "Rocky" a few minutes before I gathered everyone into my living room, where I had set up a theater-like setting. I introduced the occasion and all of the participants and described white collar boxing. Then the film began to roll. People were astounded, not only that someone went to the trouble of making a nationally televised film in which I was featured, but also by the kind of rigorous training that someone must go through to succeed in this sport. In the days following the program, I received phone calls and letters from people all over the country. People who I hadn't heard from in years called or wrote that they had seen the film and were impressed. I have always certainly realized that a few friends of mine and other acquaintances or people I would meet viewed my boxing with a jaundiced eye, and never completely understood why I did it. Many of those skeptics who hadn't taken my boxing seriously now viewed me in a different light, as they saw the level of skill and agility I had displayed in the ring.

Through this experience, I realized something else about white collar boxing: that I was in a position to help it. I was amazed by the number of my friends and clients who had no idea what the white collar boxing world (of which I was now very much a part) was really about. Most had never heard of Gleason's Gym. In the room that night were some people who probably thought of boxing as a vicious sport, with little redeeming qualities. Time and time again, I heard people exclaim "I had no idea that you had to train so hard." Or "When do you have time to do all that?" Others said, "I am so impressed that you have the discipline and determination to go through all the preparation it takes to succeed at this sport." One friend told me, "I have a new respect for the sport of boxing, having seen this." At the end of the evening, I felt really great that I had gathered all of my friends together for this happy occasion and that I had opened some people's eyes to the benefits of white collar boxing.

I realized I could contribute to white collar boxing in my own way. I would redouble my efforts to help this great sport, and this unique subset of the sport called white collar boxing. I also wanted to move my own skill level forward, as I still felt I had not yet reached my potential.

CHAPTER
9

TRAINING IS EVERYTHING

The fight is won or lost far away from witnesses—behind the lines, in the gym and out there on the road, long before I dance under those lights.
—MUHAMMAD ALI

I think the fall is a great time to train hard for a fight. There is something really special in the air, particularly in New York City. I am always amazed at how the weather in New York turns from sultry hot to pleasantly mild immediately after Labor Day. It's as if someone presses a button. I am also fortunate enough to live next to Central Park, one of the greatest parks in the world. The fall weather in Central Park is perfect running weather. And, as Bruce Lee said, "running is the king of exercise."

I personally get much more out of running outdoors than running indoors or on a treadmill. Running outdoors allows you to connect with nature and experience all of the sights and smells the world has to offer. I think that running and weight lifting are the key exercises to supplement boxing. Developing the wind and the lungs to endure a hard, strenuous exercise like a three- or four-mile run is a great backdrop for getting in fighting shape. Weight lifting can easily be done year round, but running is more problematic, due to weather conditions, at least in the Northeast. The winter months can be brutally cold and discouraging. The summer months can be too hot and sultry, and you have to fight the constant temptation to leave town on the long summer weekends. The spring is pretty, too—almost distractingly so. Give me the fall. The fall is my boxing season.

I have never done any physical exercise or sporting event in my life that demanded more preparation than a white collar sparring match. For a serious professional in the business world, this can be a great challenge. But, to short circuit the process is not an option for me. I have seen ill-prepared boxers wind up on their back, or huffing and puffing so badly at the end of the fight that it made them look like they never trained at all. My objective is to look good in the ring, demonstrate good skills, and control the fight from the opening bell. I also have a strong defensive objective—I do not like to get hit. For these reasons, I strive to take no shortcuts in the training process. That means sacrifices have to be made. I have learned to say "no" to a lot of social opportunities. I have excused myself and left parties early on many occasions. I have even arranged my calendar at work to accommodate trainers and sparring partners. So, how does a middle-aged guy train for a fight? The answer to this question is a bit more complex and convoluted than it first appears.

Most of the people I fight are in their thirties, as a rule. There are big differences between a 50-year-old and a 30-year-old. The older one gets, the tougher it is to stay in shape. This is certainly true of boxing. Again, boxing is the only Olympic sport with an age cap—34. There's a reason for this. It is a physically demanding sport, with the real possibility of getting hurt if you are ill prepared. In addition, the body becomes more vulnerable to pain as it ages. Because of the nature of the sport of boxing, its participants are more likely to be affected by these factors than other sports. For these reasons, when you reach your thirties in professional boxing, your skill level and proficiency in the sport are likely on the decline. This means you have to work even harder than your younger opponents if you want to stay "in the game." Again, the high stakes kind of boxing that's performed in the professional ranks is a far cry from the white collar sparring I do. Nevertheless, these basic principles hold true for boxing at all levels.

I have always been a firm believer in having your own equipment in a sport. There is something very comforting about athletic gear which you know is good quality and which you can rely on. It builds confidence. Boxing gear is inexpensive and easily obtained. Except for sparring, boxing gear is much the same as what you would normally wear for a gym workout. The basic equipment for a boxing workout starts with shorts, a t-shirt, sports socks, boxing shoes, and hand wraps. Due to the foot movement required to box, boxing shoes are highly recommended, either high top or low top. Personally, I prefer high top, as they give your ankles more support. When you get to the point you are ready to spar, you will need a protective cup (for men), a protective sports bra (for women), a mouthpiece, and headgear. The mouthpiece will need to be molded and shaped to the user's mouth, as described in Chapter 4, and this should be done a day or two prior to using it for the first time. Sometimes when I spar or fight, I have my hands taped in gauze, instead of using wraps—a professional trainer can guide you through this. However, a roll of white athletic tape also comes in handy to keep the strings on a glove, which usually have hard tips at the end, from causing injury to your opponent. A sturdy bag to carry this equipment is also recommended, unless you have a locker to keep it in. All of this equipment can easily be ordered over the Internet from such boxing equipment suppliers as Everlast (www.everlastboxing.com), Ringside (www.ringside.com), and Title (www.titleboxing.com). Most boxing gyms carry some equipment that is available for purchase.

Brandon Sim

*John Oden, left, trains with Brandon Sim at the
New York Athletic Club.*

Training is everything in boxing. In the following pages, I'll offer some suggestions and ideas on training, and describe methods that have worked for me, including workouts, exercise, diet, and sleep. However, I strongly recommend that anyone considering the sport hire and consult their own qualified trainer, as well as a registered nutritionist. A visit to a physician before a program is begun is also highly recommended.

One simple objective I have is to never get out of shape—it makes getting in shape that much easier. I am constantly in a mode of "maintaining," whether I am training for a fight or not. By maintaining, I mean that I visit the gym at least once a week for sparring and a boxing workout, and at least once for weights. Then I try to run outdoors at least once a week to supplement this. For this "maintaining" phase, I divide the workouts as follows:

Boxing workout (once a week)—sparring four to five rounds with my usual sparring partner, or others I may find at the New York Athletic Club on our Wednesday night workout. (A "round" is a regular professional boxing round of three minutes, timed by a bell, followed by a one minute rest period. Even though competitive white collar boxing matches are three two-minute rounds, training rounds are three minutes.) In addition to this:
- three rounds of shadow boxing in front of a mirror
- three rounds on the heavy bag (a large, bulky bag hung from the ceiling)
- three rounds on the speed bag (a smaller bag about the size of a football hung at eyesight, which is hit rapidly)
- three rounds hitting the mitts (the trainer holds two catcher's type mitts in front of the boxer to punch)
- three rounds of jump rope
- 30 push-ups (three sets of 10)
- 75 sit-ups (three sets of 25)

Weights (once or twice a week)—I perform sets of repetitions, which include:
- three sets of 10 bench presses of 125 pounds of free weights, while lying flat on my back on a flat bench
- three sets of 10 presses of 95 pounds from the shoulders, while sitting erect, to the position where my arms are fully extended, on a machine
- three sets of five to eight chin-ups on a chinning bar (very important)
- three sets of sit-ups of 25 to 50 each, 75 to 150 total, depending on method used, on a bench
- one set of body bends on a machine, from a leaning, straight position, to almost fully doubled over—3 repetitions of 15 each time for 45 total
- one set of 10 curls of 30 pounds of free weights in each hand while sitting (20 curls total)

• two sets of 10 curls of 25 pounds of free weights in each hand, while standing (20 curls total—each set)

Running (once or twice a week)—Approximately 3 miles each run in Central Park, weather permitting. This is alternated with five to six 100 to 200 meter wind sprints on an indoor track.

I also begin every day with 30 push-ups (three sets of 10) and 75 sit-ups (three sets of 25). My objective while maintaining is to work out at least three times a week—at a minimum: one boxing workout, one workout with weights, and one run, as noted above. But frequently, I can get in five workouts. This depends on many factors, including demands from the office, including travel requirements, time of the year, and weather. Sometimes weather conditions simply do not permit an outdoor workout. On the other hand, running in the snow sometimes can be fun. There is simply no excuse, however, for not doing boxing and weights in bad weather.

In addition to this, I also watch my diet. Keep in mind, I like an exquisite gourmet meal as much as anyone else. I also like fine wines and good beers. However, a few basic strategies can pay long-term dividends. My eating regimen is something that works for me. Diet is important, and doctors and nutritionists should be consulted in setting up a diet.

Stated simply, I try to eat as healthily as possible. I avoid breads and butter, as well as pizza and pasta, for example. I avoid fried foods and greasy foods like bacon. Once a week, usually on a weekend, I may drink one or two beers, or one or two glasses of wine. I drink sparkling water or seltzer all day long and throughout my meals, whether or not I am sipping a beer or a glass of wine. I eat fruit or cereal for breakfast. I use skim milk in my cereal and in my coffee. I eat yogurt and fruit for lunch, occasionally with some cottage cheese. I eat vegetables with either fish or steak for dinner. Sometimes for dinner, I eat raw vegetables; other nights the vegetables are cooked. I have never been a big dessert eater, but I inherited a love of ice cream from my mother, so when I must have it, I eat non-fat frozen yogurt. My regimen is all about what's practical, what works for me. To my diet I supplement my "maintaining" workout above, try to get as much rest as my active schedule will allow, and do the best I can to stick to my objectives of "maintaining" my physical fitness.

The reason that "maintaining" is so important is twofold—first, it is so easy to allow yourself to get out of shape. And once I am really out of shape, the road back to "fighting ready" is a long and painful one. Second, there are times when I have been asked to take fights without a lot of advance notice. Unless I am at least in a maintaining mode, doing so would be impossible.

When I am training for a competitive fight, the regimen becomes much more intense. I start at least two months in advance of the fight. I work with the same three categories, as above, but I am working out at least once a day, and frequently twice a day, as follows:

Boxing workout—three per week with up to 10 sparring rounds per workout, plus the other workout components mentioned above in the "maintaining" discussion. The boxing workouts are held:
- Wednesday nights at the New York Athletic Club
- Saturday mornings at Gleason's Gym
- One other time and place agreed upon between my trainer and me, sometimes just with him

Weights—same as above in the "maintaining" discussion, accelerated to 2 times per week

Running—up to four or five times per week, alternating between runs up to four miles, and a series of 100, 200, and 300 meter sprints. The sprints can frequently be combined with a boxing workout. Fighters do not have to be long-distance runners, but need to have good wind and the ability to last the required number of rounds. Actually, sprints are better than a long run. Sometimes instead of doing a normal run, I will do a boxer's run, meaning that for the first mile, I will run in a high skipping motion. The second mile I will run backwards. And the third mile I will run in a zigzag motion. These variations on a normal run make me use different muscles and test different agilities which I might need in an actual fight.

As you can see mathematically, I am getting up to 11 workouts per week. The runs are usually in the morning, allowing the evenings to be used for boxing and weights. Sometimes I will go to Gleason's Gym early in the morning and run across the Brooklyn Bridge and back at dawn, a distance of three miles, and then have a boxing workout, including a sparring session. This is hard to do, and means I am probably getting into the office no earlier than 9:30 or 10 A.M., which throws me behind in my day's activities. I also increase my morning exercise routine to 50 push-ups and 200 sit-ups.

Remember, this is a program that works for me. Like many activities in life, each person needs to find their own routine that works for them. Some people require more exercise than others to attain a certain level of fitness. The above program is one that I have worked out for me over the years. Each person needs to find what works for them.

I should also mention sleep. I try to arise very early, between 5:00 and 5:30 A.M. during the week, somewhat later on the weekends (usually 6:00 A.M. on Saturdays and 7:00 A.M. on Sundays). I find that is a great time for clarity of thought, and it allows for an early morning run if that is on the training schedule, while still being able to get to work on time. With my workout schedule, occasional social activities, and career demands, I find it hard to get to bed before 10:30 or 11:00 P.M., although my target is to get to bed by 10:00 P.M. during the week. I should get more sleep, but this is easier said than done. Fortunately, I do not require as much sleep as some people. There is certainly a lot to be said for getting up to eight hours of sleep of day, but I just can not do it. When possible, I try to catch up on weekends.

In addition, when preparing for a fight, I go from a healthy diet to a *very disciplined* healthy diet. In addition to the diet described above, I make the following adjustments:

- No alcoholic beverages
- No low-fat frozen yogurt
- No milk or dairy products
- Generally eat less of everything and only at "regular" hours, no late snacks

There is not much room for compromise here. I get a little boring at dinner parties, to the extent I have time to go to them. However, once you really take away all the "goodies" in a diet, I start to feel a real clarity of purpose, and I become obsessed with eating as healthfully as possible. Strange as it may sound, it becomes fun to turn away from wines, pizza, desserts. It's part of the preparation. I begin to see my body getting really sculpted and all of a sudden it becomes worth it. I am 6'4", and normally weigh about 210 pounds. However, I like to weigh under 200 pounds for a fight. As this training, diet, and discipline occurs and all these forces come together, I also see myself getting in superb shape for the fight, both mentally and physically.

In short, as the time draws nearer and nearer for a fight, I am approaching what in sports is known as the "zone," the area of mental and physical awareness created by your preparation where you are highly trained and very aware of your body and its strengths and limitations. And then the question becomes, am I ready to put all of this to the test? Have I prepared well? Have I been forced to take shortcuts which will come at a later cost?

CHAPTER

10

FIGHTING COPS, FIREMEN, SENATORS, AND HILARY SWANK

Shoot for the moon. Even if you miss it,
you will land among the stars.
—LES BROWN, MOTIVATIONAL SPEAKER AND AUTHOR

One thing I have always liked about boxing is the wide variety of people who either participate or enjoy the sport. When I meet someone who likes boxing, there is an immediate connection. That is not to say that golfers don't like other golfers; that baseball fans don't like other baseball fans, etc. But in boxing the connection is strong, immediate, and often lasting.

When I was in the army, I remember hearing my superiors say that the army was "the great equalizer." That is, it would take people from all walks of life, practically shave their heads, put them in the same drab uniform, make them march in lockstep, wake them up at the same time in the morning, feed them all the same food at the same time of day, and put them to sleep at the same time at night. No one in the army was exempt from this treatment; everyone was treated equally. When I was in the army, I did not like this treatment; I wanted my individuality. Yet, despite my feelings about that aspect of army life, white collar boxing is similar in this respect; it takes people from all backgrounds, economic circumstances, and professions, and puts them in the ring together. I actually think that boxing does this in a more profound way than most sports, due to the wide variety of people who participate in it. For example, I think that it would be fair to say that there might be a certain similarity of background by golfers at a particular country club in a particular suburb in a particular city. However, when I go to a white collar sparring match at Gleason's, I never know what type of person is working out on the heavy bag next to me, or shadow boxing in front of the mirror. Until I meet and get to know them, I can never generalize who I might be matched up with, or what their background might be. My opponents have represented a huge variety of backgrounds, professions, and circumstances. In a boxing ring, education and social status do not matter. Yet we're all connected through our passion for the sport. I have experienced this connection many times, but I want to tell you about four in particular: a fight with a policeman, a fight with a fireman, a sparring session with a senator, and yes, a rousing sparring session with the actress Hilary Swank.

The first opponent I would like to mention was a member of the New York Police Department (NYPD). The head boxing coach of the New York Athletic Club (NYAC), Dan O'Leary, was formerly the head boxing coach of the Boxing Team of the NYPD. Because of this connection, every year or so, the NYAC Boxing Team and the NYPD Boxing Team have a match. This usually causes quite a stir around the NYAC (I can't speak for the NYPD), as the policemen are viewed as tough guys, and very physically fit. They're also usually young—policemen can retire after 20 years of service, which for some is as early as the age of 40. There is mandatory retirement at age 57. All of this is also true for the New York Fire Department, which occasionally participates in these bouts. So when these matches occur, they are usually well attended and our fighters train hard for them.

As a footnote, the entire city of New York—indeed, the entire world—gained new respect for both policemen and firemen as a result of their heroic efforts during the horrific terrorist attacks in New York City on September 11, 2001. Policemen (the "finest") and firemen (the "bravest") are deeply respected by the citizens of this city, as everyone realizes the intense sacrifices which they made to protect everyone here. So, when this event was announced for October of 2002, a little over one year after the terrorist attacks of September 11, everyone felt it would be a special evening, indeed.

A couple of the guys on the Gleason's traveling team were policemen, and I had gotten to know them reasonably well on one or two of the trips we made together. One of them, Sergeant Russell Jung, had gotten my attention, because he was so good. When we were in London earlier in the year, Russell had been matched up with the best boxer on the English team, a 32-year-old boxer named Dr. Alex Mehta, who had an amateur record of 39–1 while fighting as an "Oxford Double Blue." He was also a very flashy boxer and an outspoken individual. A year earlier, Alex had been matched with Judge Phil Maier, who had great difficulty hitting Alex, since he was extremely fast and had great footwork. However, Russell held his own against Alex, and in the opinion of everyone I spoke with, had "won" the fight. (Again, in a white collar sparring match, there is no official winner or loser). Russell is an extremely talented boxer, with a martial arts background, and very fast on his feet. I was very impressed with his performance in London, and, since I was not fighting that night, I was able to film his fight.

The NYAC–NYPD fights were announced for October 10, 2002. Our coaches were comparing the two teams, and trying to make the best matches possible. At first glance, there did not seem to be a good match for me. So I called my good friend, Russell Jung, and asked him if he could help out. He thought about it for a couple of days, and called me back with the name of Dave Melin, a detective who was head of the "gang squad" in Staten Island, meaning that he led a team of undercover agents who chased gangs for a living! I thought to myself, "This will be interesting!" I was told Dave was 37 years old, about my height and weight. I passed Russell's recommendation on to our coaches and accepted the fight—too late to turn back at that point.

The night of the big fights arrived, October 10, 2002. The event was held in the NYAC gymnasium where I had fought in the NYAC championships two years earlier. The gym is a massive structure, and a daunting place to fight; it truly gives you the feeling of being completely in the spotlight. I had met Detective Melin briefly in the boxing room of the NYAC, which both teams shared, to change into our uniforms. He was slightly taller than me, had a long ponytail, and some imposing tattoos. I took one look at him and knew immediately that he worked "undercover." I also have a thing about fighting guys with tattoos. I've always felt that people with tattoos are a rough bunch—perhaps that's what they want others to think. But, again, it was too late to turn back by then.

I was the third fight, and made my way downstairs. I had trained hard with Ricky Young, but had asked one of our head coaches, Mike Fullam, a former NYAC Heavyweight Champion, to be in my corner, since this was an official NYAC fight. However, Ricky was there, offering me moral support. I heard my teammate, Patrick Ledford, being announced as the winner of the fight before mine. Unlike true white collar sparring, this was a challenge match between two teams, and each fight had a winner and a loser. I made my way to the ring and climbed up and in.

The atmosphere was electric, and the room was well lit. There was a lot of background noise from a restless crowd, many of whom were policemen and firemen. I did my normal "ring dance," which is something Ricky Young taught me. When I enter the ring, I immediately move quickly to all four corners of the ring, testing the ropes by bouncing off of them, measuring my footing in the ring and the base of the ring we are standing on by jogging around on it. These actions, simple as they may seem, make a strong impression on everyone who sees me, including my opponent, before the fight begins. It makes me look—and feel—more confident.

I saw that the referee was Arthur Mercante, Jr., the son of one of the most famous referees of all time and a NYAC member, Arthur Mercante. Arthur, Jr., is an excellent professional referee in his own right, and I was glad he was in the ring with me that night. It was Arthur, Jr., who refereed both of the heavyweight world championship matches between Lennox Lewis and Evander Holyfield in 1999. I felt fortunate to have such professionalism beside me. Arthur briefly reviewed the rules, and the bell rang.

Detective Melin was a very big guy, and had an extremely annoying jab, which he kept sticking in my face. I got through the first round okay, and felt good. He came on solidly in the second round. I rallied hard in the third round, and was convinced that I had piled up enough points to win. There is a very definite system to scoring points in a fight, and it is a mathematical calculation for the most part, although there is some subjectivity involved. For example, a clean hit to the head or body is one point, and a knockdown is one point. Then if it is a close fight, more subjectively judged criteria, such as how the fighters handle themselves in the ring, whether they keep their mouthpieces in, and how they move around the ring and display confidence, are taken into account. Points can also be deducted for low blows and unsportsmanlike conduct. Once everything is tallied, the fighter with the highest number of points wins. A knockout erases the point system, and a winner is immediately declared, regardless of who was ahead at the time of the knockout. However, when the points were tallied on this fight with

Detective Melin, his name was announced as the winner. Nevertheless, it was a good close fight. I give two accounts of the fight for the records:

From Doug Harden of the *Spitbucket News*, which I had not heretofore heard of:

> *Most of the guys cracked a smile. One who didn't was a tall lanky heavyweight named John Oden. He was very quiet and seemed a bit nervous. "Probably his first fight" I said to myself. I know because I've been there too. The nervousness is brought more on by not looking good in front of your family and friends than actually getting hit. That's why I say orphans make good boxers.*
>
> *His opponent was Det. Dave Melin, Staten Island. He wore his hair in a ponytail and his upper arms were decorated with tattoos. If this was one of those B biker movies, Melin would be the bad guy and Oden the sheriff but up in the ring it was a different story. The first minute of the opening round both boxers felt each other out with long jabs. Melin appeared to be the stronger fighter, but Oden was the smarter of the two. When Melin would start to attack, Oden would jab setting off Melin's rushes or he would tie him up and punch free. In the second Oden growing more confident began taking the fight to Melin, using the jab the way an offensive front line creates openings for a quarterback Once the punch created daylight, BOOM, right hand to the jaw. In the third both fighters showed good condition with good infighting. Oden got the better of the exchanges and the decision.*

This writer thought I had won. How could the *Spitbucket News* be wrong? God bless him! I later learned that Doug is a writer for *Boxing Digest,* and uses the *Spitbucket News* for his press releases. Now I was really impressed. In essence, *Boxing Digest,* through one of its freelance writers, Doug Harden, thought I won the fight. My father would have been thrilled, had he been alive.

For another opinion, the NYAC *Winged Foot*, December 2002 issue, had this to say:

> The third match featured John "Pecos Kid" Oden against Detective Dave Melin of the NYPD's Staten Island Gang Division. Melin looked every bit the part of the undercover detective he is, complete with a torso covered in tattoos and scars. If one were to judge this contest strictly on appearances, Melin had a seemingly easy night ahead of him. Such was not the case. Oden, a Club veteran, used his experience and finely refined skills to consistently beat Melin to the punch, keeping the detective off balance and tying him up on the inside. In a surprising decision, the judges saw this fight differently, and Melin was declared the winner.

These two writeups convinced me that I did a good job that night. The verdict just didn't go my way. But what a terrific experience. Detective Melin and I had a great time after the fight, as the NYAC hosted the NYPD for a nice dinner at the club. We had fun talking about the fight and introducing each other to our friends. Videos of all the fights that night were shown continuously throughout our dinner. I have received reports from friends of mine, and other boxers on the NYAC team who have seen him at fights around the city, that he always asks about me. When I meet other policemen, who frequently work out with the NYAC Boxing Team, I always ask about him. What an opportunity this was to get to know someone who lives a life considerably different than mine, and to bond with him in very special way.

In the summer of 2003, Gleason's Gym announced its first ever "Fantasy Boxing Camp." Bruce Silverglade added the

"Fantasy" because a traditional boxing camp is for professional boxers only, not white collar boxers. Muhammad Ali, for example, often sequestered himself in a boxing camp out in a secluded country location weeks before a fight, where he'd train hard, spar, do roadwork, and follow a strict diet while preparing for the upcoming match. The Gleason's camp was the first boxing camp ever offered to white collar boxers. It was scheduled at Kutsher's Country Club in Monticello, New York, in the Catskill Mountains, for four days, October 16–19, 2003. Gleason's billed it as an opportunity to experience the reality of a real training camp within the comforts of an exclusive country club. The camp offered an intensive four-day training schedule, during which each boxer would have the opportunity to train with current and past world champions— among them, Juan Laporte, Matthew Said Muhammad, Carlos Ortiz, Mark Breland, and Emile Griffith. A white collar sparring match was planned for Saturday evening, with all attendees encouraged to participate. Approximately 23 fighters attended, along with 8 trainers, most of them former world champion trainers—a very good fighter/trainer ratio.

The camp started Thursday morning, October 16. Unfortunately, I was unable to show up until Friday afternoon, but jumped right into the fray. The format for the camp was an early morning three-mile run, followed by breakfast and then a two-hour workout beginning at 8:30 A.M., including sparring. Following lunch, there was usually a boxing lecture, followed by a two-hour afternoon workout. We had dinner at 5 P.M., and a three-mile evening run at 7 P.M. It was really terrific. I got to know all of the past world champions, and most of the boxers.

For the matches on Saturday night, I was matched up with Patrick O'Lear, a fireman from Detroit. Pat weighed in at a solid 250 pounds, which was about 20 percent more than I weighed at the time! Stated bluntly, he was a mountain of a man, really huge and menacing looking with his gear on, and

Portrait of John "The Pecos Kid" Oden by the legendary artist Al Hirschfeld.

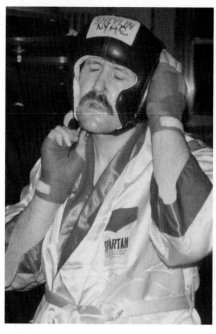

Oden's first opponent, Scott "Slick" Butler, gets ready for their fight at the New York Athletic Club in 1993.

Oden's trainer, Ronnie Cecchetti, gives him a water break during a match at the Downtown Athletic Club in 1995.

Oden with Gerry Cooney after a Saturday morning sparring session in 2004.

Julie Skarratt

Oden, on the right, leads with the jab in his fight against John Turco at the Downtown Athletic Club in 1996.

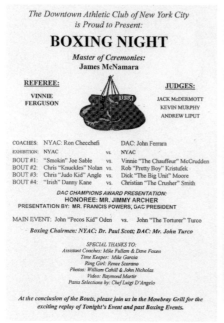

Julie Skarratt

The fight card for the New York Athletic Club-Downtown Athletic Club Boxing Night features John "The Pecos Kid" Oden versus John "The Torturer" Turco as the main event.

Former World Heavyweight Champion "Smokin'" Joe Frazier gives Oden his medal at the NYAC-DAC bouts.

Bruce Silverglade, center, invites David Lawrence, left, one of the original white collar boxers, and Ricky Young, right, a trainer, into his memorabilia-lined office.

Julie Skarratt

Fighters from a Friday "White Collar Sparring Night" at Gleason's Gym in 1997 include: (back row, from left to right) two unidentified men, Yiyo Guzman, Craig "Farang Ba" Wilson, John Oden, Yelena Binder, Bill Hunnicutt, Zoel Daschuta, Bob Jackson (in glasses), Bobby Babilonia, Carlos Sanchez, Sr., Bill Logan (holding trophy), Frank Shattuck, Jack Kendrick; (front row) Tommy Ryan, Tony Pellegrino, Darius Ford, Dominic Monaco.

The NYAC Boxing Team that Oden brought to Gleason's in 1997: Craig "Farang Ba" Wilson, Bill "Hurricane" Hunnicutt, Jack "The Dancing Ghost" Kendrick, John "The Pecos Kid" Oden, Tommy Ryan, and Dave Foxen. Craig Wilson was making one of his last appearances for the NYAC team before moving to Thailand.

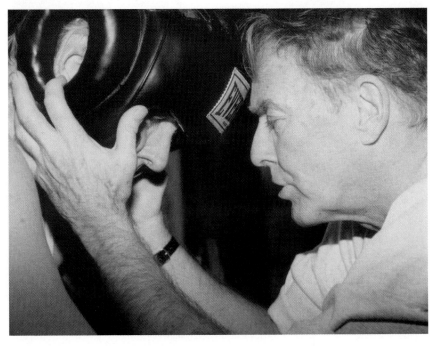

Oden is "in the zone" with Jack Kendrick at Gleason's Gym in 1997.

Oden, on the left, jabs Detective Dave Melin at the NYAC versus New York Police Department bouts in 2002.

New York State Senator Joseph Bruno, on the left, spars with Oden at Gleason's Gym in 2003, with Gerry Cooney (on the right) refereeing.

Oden, on the left, squares off with Mark Settembre at a White Collar Sparring Night at Gleason's Gym in 2000. Earlier that year, Oden had defeated Settembre at the New York Athletic Club Championships.

Oden, left, spars with Hilary Swank during her training for the movie *Million Dollar Baby*.

Oden compares post-sparring strategy with Hilary Swank at Gleason's Gym in 2004.

Oden, right, and his frequent sparring partner, Chris Angle, coached by Emanuel Steward, work out at the New York Athletic Club in 2004.

Emanuel Steward demonstrates defensive moves to Oden the week before Hedge Fund Fight Night.

Oden is announced by Alan Lacey of The Real Fight Club as he weighs in for Hedge Fund Fight Night in London in 2004.

Oden warms up in the mirror for Hedge Fund Fight Night.

Emanuel Steward, Oden, referee Loui Wyatt, Gray Smith, and Smith's trainer Keith Wilson gather for the moment of truth at the start of the fight.

Christina Beckles, on the right, punches Maria Vasquez at the Golden Gloves finals at Madison Square Garden in April 2005. Christina won the gold medal in the women's 101–pound class that night.

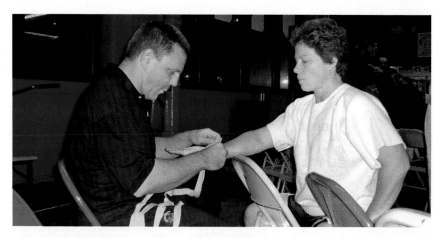

Trainer John Spehar, left, wraps Dr. Samantha Dane's hands.

Hector Roca, who trained Hilary Swank for her role in *Million Dollar Baby*, shows a woman at Gleason's how to wrap her hand.

From left to right, Louis Torres, Principal Intern at I.S. #174; Frank Martinez, Chief Referee, USA Boxing Metro; Matthew Ruggero, Director of New York Public School Boxing at I.S. #174/John E. Oden Boxing Scholars; Oden; Brandon Sim; Nikos Spanakos; and Pete Spanakos, pose with students at I.S. #174 in the Bronx.

Oden, Ken Norton, and Gerry Cooney attend the 2004 benefit dinner for F.I.S.T. Fights for New York.

John Oden, "The Pecos Kid," at Gleason's Gym.

very strong. However, he was a relatively inexperienced fighter. Nonetheless, as Carlos Ortiz told me, "Any big guy who hits you can hurt you." We had a good, crisp match, and I kept my jab in front of him most of the time to prevent him from getting close to me. Sometimes first-time fighters can be very dangerous because they swing wildly and with abandon. Patrick was more controlled, thankfully, and I just kept sticking him with my jab. On one occasion, however, he clubbed me in the chest with a big right hand. I shook it off, but I definitely felt it. Former WBC featherweight champion Juan Laporte was the referee and former WBA light heavyweight champion Matthew Said Muhammad was in my corner. Can't beat that! Afterwards, there was a party to celebrate the matches, and I spend a lot of time with Patrick and his wife, who had driven from Michigan to participate in the Gleason's camp. He had found out about the camp on the Internet, and thought it would be a good experience. Patrick and I have been in touch many times since, remain friends, and correspond on occasion. Gleason's Fantasy Boxing Camp grew in the second year, with 31 fighters. Bruce is planning a third year in 2005.

I am hardly a political person. People are constantly asking me if I am a Republican or a Democrat. I always reply that I am a capitalist. In reality, I vote my pocketbook every time.

Sometime in 2003, I was introduced to the New York State Senate Majority Leader, Joseph Bruno. I had hosted a reception earlier in the year in my apartment for U.S. Senator Lindsey Graham of South Carolina, and was later approached by friends of Senator Bruno to do the same for him. As I did not know Senator Bruno, I told his associates that I would need to meet the senator and spend a little time with him. I had to feel that he and I had enough in common that it was appropriate to invite people into my home to meet him.

It was arranged that I would meet him at his hotel suite one afternoon in July. I was greeted by the senator and several members of his executive staff. We sat down, and the senator had really done his homework. He knew a lot about me, including the fact that I boxed. When the subject of boxing came up, the senator and I immediately bonded. He shared the fact that he was the Light Heavyweight Boxing Champion in the U.S. Army in the Korean War, 25th Army Division. Further, he was undefeated and weighed three pounds less now than when he was winning boxing titles back in the 1950s. He had a great deal of pride about his boxing, and we spoke about his boxing career, my boxing career, and boxing in general at great length. The bonding was complete. I agreed to host the reception, and the senator and I began a relationship that has continued to develop ever since.

After spending time with the senator on a number of occasions, I asked him if he might be interested in a tour of Gleason's Gym and maybe a workout, as he had never been there. He did not respond at first, and I gathered that he wanted to check on his medical progress (he was combatting prostate cancer, and really fighting it hard) before committing to something that strenuous. After some discussion, we set a date to meet at Gleason's on October 22, 2003. I arranged a luncheon that day in the area around Gleason's, which is called DUMBO (Down Under the Manhattan Bridge Overpass—Gleason's is actually near the Brooklyn Bridge). DUMBO is an area of New York City that is developing very quickly, with a lot of nice restaurants and residential developments. I really wanted to introduce Bruce Silverglade and Senator Bruno for a number of reasons, including the fact that I like both of them very much. But I also hoped that Senator Bruno might think of a way to be helpful to Gleason's.

The senator arrived in his helicopter, and I met him and his executive staff. We were whisked down to the DUMBO area, and met Bruce at the restaurant. The senator had a few members of his executive staff with him, and I had also invited my friend, Judge Phil Maier, in case the senator wanted to spar. I had brought my gym bag with me, and was ready to spar with the senator if he felt like it—it was really the senator's decision. I had also invited "Gentleman" Gerry Cooney, the former #1 heavyweight contender who fought Larry Holmes for the Heavyweight Championship of the World in 1982, to meet us at the gym, as Gerry and the senator knew each other. I also thought Gerry would be a great referee if we decided to spar.

Our lunch went well, and off we went to Gleason's. The senator did not hesitate. After a tour of Gleason's by Bruce Silverglade, the senator went straight to the locker room, and changed into his boxing gear. The senator climbed into the famed center ring at Gleason's. Phil Maier was there waiting for him. I had suggested that Phil spar with the senator first, as the senator weighed around 174, and Phil weighed around 150. Since it had been a while since the senator had sparred, I thought that it might give him some confidence to go against Phil for a round or two.

Several other senators showed up. Three television networks showed up, as well as several newspapers, to cover the event. Gerry Cooney was in the ring, as was Phil Maier. The bell rang, and they went at it. Phil fought very defensively, but the senator showed great form. People at the gym loved it. They had a good round of boxing.

For the second round, I climbed in the ring and Phil climbed out. When the bell rang, the senator came right at me. I used my jab, and kept him away for the most part. We had a good round, and the bell rang. I looked over at the senator and asked if he would like another round. He nodded his head. The bell rang again, and this time the senator moved right to me. He caught me with one really good shot, which of course, was carried by all three networks covering the match! For the most part, I used my jab, kept him away, and we had a great time.

The October 23, 2003 edition of *The New York Sun* carried this story about the time which Senator Bruno and I spent together at Gleason's:

*The next contender—John Oden, a money manager
for Alliance Capital—put up a good fight, connecting
more than once. After the match, Mr. Oden confessed that
although he trains every day, he found the senator a "formidable opponent." "This guy is a heavyweight, and I'm
a light-heavy," said a flushed Mr. Bruno after the match.
His skills from a brief stint as a boxer in Korea half a
century ago seemed to come back naturally.*

Later that night, the senator took me to a political event
which he was hosting for a group of lobbyists. This is apparently
an annual event, and was very well attended. The senator
announced that he and I had been sparring earlier at Gleason's.
I am sure I beamed with pride. Since that time, the senator has
been in my home and I have been in his. I have introduced him
to many friends of mine, who have an interest in politics, and
have even given him a political fundraiser, a first for me. Again,
it is unlikely that the senator and I would ever have connected
in such a major way without the bonding we experienced
through boxing.

On the final night of the 2004 New York Golden Gloves
finals at Madison Square Garden on April 16, 2004, I was sitting in the upper deck, and looked down at the crowd below.
I saw a crowd of people I knew at the level on the first set of
rows just above ringside. In the group were Bruce and JoEllen
Silverglade, and some Gleason's regulars, Perry D'Alessio,
Frank Shattuck, Phil Maier, and a trainer from Gleason's,
Hector Roca. Between fights I wandered down. I was pulled
into a seat by Perry D'Alessio, and began watching the fights
from that new vantage point. In the middle of this crowd, sitting in the row directly in front of me, was an attractive
woman, in the middle of two men. She was quite animated,
and was enjoying the fights a great deal. I learned from Perry
D'Alessio that this woman was Hilary Swank, and she was

with her husband, Chad Lowe, and her father, Steve Swank. She had been training at Gleason's Gym for a movie she was about to make entitled *Million Dollar Baby*, a story about a woman living in a trailer park (played by Hilary Swank), who meets two aging former boxers who are now boxing trainers (Clint Eastwood and Morgan Freeman), and winds up as a boxer in the hopes of improving her life. Between fights, she turned around and introduced herself, as did Chad Lowe. I was most favorably impressed.

At this point, Hilary was already well known to the Gleason's regulars. She was extremely pleasant to be around, exceedingly polite and respectful, and very friendly. Hector Roca, a regular trainer at Gleason's, introduced me to her, as he was the person appointed by Bruce Silverglade to oversee her training and preparation. She had planned to work out the following Saturday morning at Gleason's with my friend, Phil Maier, who I knew would be a great sparring partner for her because of his size (she is about 5'4" and 110 pounds) and his gentlemanly approach to the sport. I decided I would check this out for myself, and went down to Gleason's the next day (Saturday morning) for a workout.

By the time Hilary, her husband, and her father had arrived, I was well along in my Saturday morning routine. Phil Maier had probably sparred ten rounds by the time Hilary and her group arrived around eleven o'clock. However, after she suited up and warmed up, she and Phil sparred three good rounds, and she showed amazing form and fluidity for someone who had been boxing less than a month. After she and Phil finished their session, she did a few rounds with another woman, and then a couple of rounds with her husband. She was in no rush to hurry her workout, and everyone around her was impressed with her progress and the way she conducted herself in the gym. At one point I was going to spar with my friend Dimitri Feygin, a native of Russia who is a regular at Gleason's and one of my usual sparring partners.

Hector bumped us to allow Hilary to spar two more rounds with someone, and she thanked us afterwards for letting her go ahead of us. I was impressed with her politeness and affability, as I am by so many of the people I meet in boxing. But because this was THE Hilary Swank, an extremely successful and well-known Hollywood actress, it made a particular impression on me. It was also about the time that *People* came out with its list of the "50 Most Beautiful People" of 2004 and she was listed as one of them. (She also made the list the following year.) I also got the sense that morning that she respected Gleason's and everything it stood for, and was as awed by the legends of the boxing ring as everyone else who came there.

I returned one Saturday morning three weeks later, and as I was getting ready for my workout, I again ran into Hilary, who remembered me. We had a pleasant visit. We spoke for a while and I asked her if she had made any arrangements to spar. I told her I would be happy to move in the ring with her for a couple of rounds, if she didn't have things already planned. She checked with her trainer, Hector Roca, and he said that she could spar two rounds with me after she worked with someone else for two rounds.

Hilary had two rounds with a very good female boxer whom I had not seen before. Then we climbed into the ring together. The bell rang, and to my surprise, she came at me with full force. She moved very well, very fast, and was very serious about her game. She backed me into a corner at one point, while I used the Muhammad Ali technique of "rope-a-dope" (covering up my face and chest with my arms, while leaning on the ropes); however, she did not let up for a second and threw a couple of nice hooks, which made me realize the best strategy was to spin out of the corner and move away from her. But as I moved, she cut me off. My instincts took over, and I let go a big right hand. This was the last thing I had intended to do, but some things a fighter can't control. I hit her pretty solidly in the nose. I then realized, I just hit Hilary Swank! I stopped and apologized; later, we had our photographs taken, and she had a "red" nose. She shook it off, and if I hurt her, she did not mention it. We kept right on sparring. She had a very interesting move in which she would wind up to punch, in almost a "showboating" manner, but then finish the maneuver by delivering a nice, hard, straight punch. She moved a lot, and really kept me on my toes. I kept her away with my jab, but if I had not had that weapon, she would have been right on me, punching away. It was a good hard sparring session, and we both thought it was a good workout. We thanked each other, and I told her she was "ready." She knew I was telling the truth.

The success of the movie *Million Dollar Baby* is now well known, and the name of Hilary Swank is a household word in this country and in many places around the world. Although she had never boxed before, Hilary was a fixture at Gleason's six days a week while training for the role. "I personally found boxing to be one of the most intense workouts I think I've ever encountered," Hilary told me. "The first time I sparred, I remember thinking, 'three minutes—I'm going to kick someone's ass.' A minute and a half into it, it was all I could do to keep from getting my ass kicked. Three minutes of boxing proved I was wrong. It felt like an hour. I would say it's not only a physical workout, but also a major mental workout. It's an all-around mind/body exercise and very humbling."

I returned to the Golden Gloves finals at Madison Square Garden on the final night of the fights, Friday, April 8, 2005, and found myself seated at ringside in the press section, thanks to my friend, Pete Spanakos. When I noticed the television cameras whirring and everyone looking my way, I turned around, and saw Hilary Swank and Chad Lowe sit down in the seats on the row immediately behind me. They were coming to watch one of the sparring partners who had helped her train for *Million Dollar Baby*, Maureen Shea, a 24-year-old student from the Bronx. Maureen lost a close decision in the 125-pound weight class to Ronica Jeffrey, a nursing student and also a Gleason's regular. Hilary went to Maureen's corner between rounds to give her words of encouragement, and left immediately after her loss was announced to comfort her in her dressing room. I had gotten to know Hilary and Chad during the year that had passed and marveled to myself at the fact that we had sat next to each other for two consecutive years at the Golden Gloves finals. I was very pleased to see that she was continuing to follow her boxing, as by this time, *Million Dollar Baby* was a huge success, having won the Academy Award for Best Picture and Hilary for Best Actress.

Clearly disappointed by her friend's loss that night, Hilary nevertheless believes that boxing is a great sport for women. "I feel boxing is not a gender-specific sport. If a person has a dream and it involves boxing, they should go for it with every ounce of themselves. I met women boxers who inspired me, not only to push myself harder, but also to help me break barriers that I didn't know I could. The power and endurance of a person is regulated by the mind. I was reminded of this daily while training. Boxing may be considered a violent sport, but a person should be allowed to box if it's his or her choice." Shades of Maggie Fitzgerald (Hilary's character in *Million Dollar Baby)*! Hilary would like to continue boxing, although she acknowledges that her time schedule will not allow the six days a week training she was doing for the film.

These are four random stories, each as different as daylight and dark. I had a terrific time with each of them. Every time I realize that I actually boxed Hilary Swank, I smile to myself. It was not only her star power that intrigued me, although that certainly added to the fun of it. However, through my recent experiences at the Golden Gloves and with Hilary Swank, I have realized that women are making great progress in the sport, at least in this part of the world. But how widespread a phenomenon is this, how accepted is it, and can it continue?

CHAPTER 11

WOMEN ARE WELCOME!

*The world's an oyster and you're a pearl. Pearls
are pretty and they're tough. And pretty tough can
do anything.*
—AS TOLD TO BOXING JOURNALIST AND MANAGER JACKIE KALLEN
(MEG RYAN) BY HER UNCLE, RAY KALLEN (SEAN BELL), IN THE MOVIE
AGAINST THE ROPES

As I plowed through the volumes of Egan's *Boxiana* and
Liebling's *Sweet Science,* I looked for any reference to
women in boxing. I could find none. For most of its history,
boxing has been a very chauvinistic sport. As I looked at many
paintings and drawings of boxing matches in eighteenth century England, I observed that not only the participants, but
even the spectators, were male. Throngs of women were on
hand at some of history's biggest matches of the twentieth
century, though, judging from old photographs and film clips,
and certainly, a fair share of the boxing audiences today are
comprised of the fairer sex, frequently fashionably dressed.
Women's boxing first appeared in the Olympic Games as a
demonstration bout in 1904. It has yet to reappear.

In the ranks of white collar boxing, things have "absolutely picked up," according to Bruce Silverglade. Women boxing can be found not only in Gleason's but in other gyms around the country and the world. Gleason's has been eager to open its doors to "half the world's population," as Bruce puts it. Bruce commented that his late partner, Ira Becker, never understood women in the gym, but Bruce has always promoted the participation of women in the sport and his efforts are paying off. Women currently constitute over 20 percent of the membership of Gleason's Gym. What's more, the caliber of the women is terrific. He feels that many women are good athletes and boxers, and have a talent for the sport.

Women have been established in the amateur boxing ranks since 1993, when women's boxing recorded its first officially recognized competitive match. In that year, following a lawsuit filed by Dallas Malloy, a 16-year-old woman from Bellingham, Washington, USA Boxing officially lifted its ban on women's boxing. In October of 1993, the first women's sanctioned amateur bout took place later as Malloy won a decision over Heather Poyner in Lynnwood, Washington.

Women are now a large part of USA Boxing and can compete in sanctioned amateur competition within this country and abroad. According to the website of USA Boxing in 2005, there were almost 2,000 amateur female boxers registered with the organization. Rules regarding women's boxing are similar to the men's program with a few minor differences, which are mostly practical and logical considerations. These include the use of breast protectors instead of cups and a required waiver stating that the participant is not pregnant at the time of competition.

In 1997, USA Boxing hosted the first-ever Women's National Championships in Augusta, Georgia. Sixty-six women competed in this historic event. The second Women's National Championships in Anaheim, California, drew over 100 boxers. Since then, not only are the number of women amateur boxers been growing rapidly in the U.S., there is a dramatic increase in female boxing numbers around the world, with 34 countries worldwide having a recognized female boxing program at the amateur level.

Certainly, men and women are physically different. Bruce Silverglade feels that up to the 105 to 110-pound range, women are competitive with men, power-wise. From 120 pounds and up, however, the differences become more pronounced; he feels that men are superior at these weights. With these considerations in mind, amateur boxing has published a revised series of weight classifications for men and women. Instead of the old weight classes, which were established with names, such as lightweight, welterweight, and heavyweight, the new

MEN	WOMEN
106	101
112	106
119	110
125	114
132	119
141	125
152	132
165	138
178	145
201	154
201+	165
	176
	189
	189+ (note this category is only for USA domestic competition, otherwise women can not compete over this weight limit)

weight classes are established by maximum weight. There are 11 weight classes for men, recently reduced from 12, and 14 for women, as listed in the box.

In Golden Gloves boxing, men have two classes of boxers for each weight class—"novice" and "open." "Novice" boxers are fighters who have had between zero and nine sanctioned fights. A sanctioned fight is a fight for which the necessary requirements have been met and approvals obtained from USA Boxing. "Open" class boxers have had ten or more Golden Gloves fights, or have won a Golden Gloves tournament in Novice class. Another way to move from novice class to open class in Golden Gloves is to win another qualified amateur tournament, such as one sponsored by the Police Athletic League, Ringside, or others. Women do not have this distinction between novice and open classes; rather, there is only one category of boxer for each weight class.

As I mentioned previously, on April 15-16, 2004, I attended the 77th annual New York City Metropolitan Golden Gloves Championships, held at Madison Square Garden in New York City. This tournament was well attended, and all weight classes mentioned above except one (whose opponent didn't show up) were represented for the men in both the novice and open classes. As there are 11 separate weight classes for men, with two fights per weight class (novice and open), there were 22 fights scheduled, 21 of which were actually fought. In the women's division, for some reason, three weight classes were not represented so there were 11 fights in all. So in summary, there were 33 fights in all, 21 for the men and 11 for the women. Not a bad showing for the women in terms of numbers of fights and representation, I would say.

I had not been to a Golden Gloves finals in a few years. I recalled some matches of women I saw in previous years. I must admit I did not find them that interesting, or the talent of the boxers that good. I remember a lot of flailing punches, poor balance and uninteresting exhibitions. Was I in for a surprise!

In my friend Bert Sugar's book *Bert Sugar On Boxing*, he writes a chapter entitled "I'd Rather Poke My Eye Out With a Sharp Stick Than Watch Women's Boxing." Bert goes on to say, in his wry fashion that has made him so famous, that he just doesn't feel that women's boxing is on the same level as men's boxing, and that he has trouble taking it with any degree of seriousness.

I must admit that over the early years of women's boxing, I felt the same way. However, at the Golden Gloves finals in 2004, for the most part, the matches between women were excellent, very competitive, and the women displayed terrific boxing style, talent, and skill. What a difference a few years has made in women's boxing! The matches were fairly even for the most part, and very hard fought. On April 15, I watched the match between Jean Martin, 33, a veteran NYPD detective who went into the fight as the four-time champion and Katheryn Hutchins, 30, who was in her first final. Both boxers were skilled, but Jean Martin took it to Katheryn Hutchins from the beginning, swinging hard with straight punches and hooks, and the fight was ruled a TKO in the second round. They were fighting in the 145-pound division, and I remember being glad I wasn't in the ring with Detective Jean Martin, even though she is smaller than me. I also remember thinking that you don't get to be a four-time champion in this sport by accident.

My friend, Christina Beckles, then 33, who works with Bruce Silverglade at Gleason's Gym, fought a tough fight on April 15, 2004, in the 106-pound division against Suszannah Warner, 33. I thought Chris won the first round, but the other two rounds were close, and Suszannah got the decision. I returned to the Golden Gloves Finals on April 8, 2005, and was pleased to see Christina, then 34, avenge this loss in the 101-pound class, with an impressive victory over scrappy Maria Vasquez, 25, of Brooklyn. Christina was in top form for this fight, and took the fight to Maria from the beginning. I actually thought the fight might have been stopped, or at least

Maria should have been given a "standing 8 count" when Christina knocked Maria's mouthpiece out in the third round of their four round fight. (A standing 8 count is administered to a fighter who is in trouble in a fight, to give the fighter a short rest and make sure that the fighter is not injured so badly that the fight should not continue). In winning this fight, Christina won the gold medal in the women's 101-pound class.

As I've said before, boxing attracts unique personalities from all walks of life. This is equally true for both men and women. Let me give some examples from the women's side.

GISELE HELDT, ATTORNEY AT LAW

Gisele is an attorney in her early thirties in New York City. Formerly a litigator, she is now a transactional attorney whose clients are insurance companies. Gisele began boxing as a way to get in shape for an extended trekking trip in the Andes Mountains. She wanted to prepare for this trip by doing something truly difficult, something she had not done before, that would hold her interest. She chose boxing because of the focus it required, and the individual nature of the sport. She found that her method of training for her trek in the Andes (boxing) soon superseded her interest in the trek! She also found that her disposition at the office is now more even than before she started boxing. As a litigator, in particular, she found that she could occasionally feel intimidated and become rattled. This happens much less frequently since she found the boxing gym.

Gisele is interested in boxing because she found herself thinking about it all the time, and found that "it does not get old," as some sports tend to do after a while. She now trains six days a week—good thing she lives two blocks from the Trinity Boxing Club in New York City, where she trains. "Boxing continually surprises me," she says. Gisele finds it a very stressful sport, because of the intensity involved, much more stressful than anything she had done previously, including the bar exam. She also finds that the learning curve is as steep now as when she first started. This is not an uncommon feeling amongst boxers. One boxer friend of mine once said, "The more I learn, I realize the more I have to learn." This has to do with the fact that boxing is much more difficult than it looks, and a boxer, to be successful and display talent and skill, has a long road to climb. The road to achievement in boxing is a long one for anyone interested in the sport, and paved with many challenges along the way.

Gisele weighs 117 pounds and is 5'3" tall. She has had two white collar bouts. The first bout was against a very experienced fighter, and she was tagged by her opponent with a couple of hooks. Gisele was disappointed that she did not do better, but she had not sparred at all until three weeks before this first match. She was determined to do better.

Her second match was at Gleason's with a lefty. It was an even match-up in weight, experience, and fitness. In this fight, she learned to fight a lefty by moving to her left and leading with her right—a technique often used by right-handed fighters to combat a left-handed fighter. She felt much better about this fight, but could have thrown a lot more punches. She is planning future bouts and training hard for them.

Gisele pointed out to me that she sees differences in the way men approach the sport, versus women. She stated that men will try different things in a boxing workout. For example, a man will not be afraid to try an uppercut, just because he hasn't tried one before. On the other hand, women try to perfect a given punch, before experimenting with other punches. These are insightful observations by this up-and-coming pugilist, Gisele Heldt.

DR. SAMANTHA DANE

One person I have gotten to know at Gleason's Gym is Dr. Samantha Dane. Dr. Dane is a mid-forties, 5'1" practicing physician, who happens to be a white collar boxer. Her "day job" is as a physician in the emergency room of St.Vincent's Medical Center in Bridgeport, Connecticut. Samantha grew up in Alaska, where she participated actively in sports, including sprinting on the track team and playing volleyball and basketball. She played soccer at Seattle University, graduating with a nursing degree, then went on to become a doctor. She began boxing workouts in Rochester, where she graduated from the University of Rochester Medical School in 1996. After moving to Connecticut, Samantha had been golfing and doing other forms of exercise, when she met a trainer she really liked, John Spehar. According to Samantha, John is a charismatic guy, with whom she enjoyed working. John had a background in the martial arts. She began participating in physical fitness classes which he held as often as five days a week. Samantha often works out at the end of the day, as she works on ten hour shifts at the hospital. She is not a "morning athlete," and because of the demands of her profession, it is better for her to work out in the evening.

In 2000, Samantha began boxing workouts as a stress reliever, and eventually sparred. She "fell in love" with the sport. The more she worked out, the more she found that she wanted to compete. Finally, she agreed to try a white collar sparring night at Gleason's. The first one was tough, as she was fighting a more experienced fighter—a fighter who was at least six feet tall and later turned pro. Yet, she hung in there, concentrating on fundamentals, and did fine. She has now had four fights, and is more intrigued with the sport than ever. She finds herself improving with every fight. She has had a lot of good coaching from John Spehar, and works hard on her strategy of getting inside and going to the body, as many smaller fighters do.

Interestingly, Samantha says that most of her good friends are somehow connected with the sport. Along the way, she received one of boxing's badges of courage, a black eye. This was the subject of much teasing at the medical center where she works. People were astonished when they realized how she acquired it.

Dr. Dane is ready for her next challenge, and training hard for it. The actual scheduling of a fight is difficult, due to her demanding profession. However, that is the beauty of Gleason's Gym. All one has to do is train hard and show up at the once-a-month white collar sparring show. There are many women opponents there to choose from, as anyone who visits will see.

ANNE PARISIO, BRITISH FILMMAKER

Among the most unique female white collar boxers I have encountered is Anne Parisio, a 39-year-old filmmaker in London, who has been boxing ever since she met Alan Lacey of The Real Fight Club a few years ago. Anne has been making films for 14 or 15 years. She grew up in Essex, outside of London, and was educated in fine arts. She went back to school and graduated from the National Film School in London. She has made about 25 films, which she describes as broadcast films, which are documentaries or socially responsible films, including human interest stories, films about music, films on countries in chaos and transition, such as Haiti. These movies have been produced on national television and HBO.

White collar boxing has been extremely successful in London, but the sport simply has not caught on with women. This is hard to explain, because boxing is a very popular sport in England, and has a long history there. But it is a male-dominated sport in the white collar, amateur, and professional ranks. This makes Anne Parisio all the more unique.

Anne had a severe motorbike accident twelve years ago. She smashed both knees, and surgeons felt at the time that she would not regain her mobility. This made her realize that she could not depend on her natural strength and fitness to remain as physically fit as she would like. She was looking for ways to work out and stay in shape, but did not particularly care for the regular workouts at health and fitness centers. About this time she met Alan Lacey of The Real Fight Club. He was putting together the first challenge match between The Real Fight Club and Gleason's Gym, in May of 2000. Anne attended these bouts, which were held at Gleason's Gym, and filmed them. She thought the fights were fantastic! And she thought that Gleason's was the most fantastic place ever. She was impressed with the mix of people from all walks of life, as well as the strong cadre of professional people who were in attendance that evening.

Following this experience, she began training at early morning workouts with my friend, Adrian Dodson, at Kronk Boxing Gym in London. At the same time, Alan Lacey began organizing group sessions, which she joined on occasion. She began to spar, and found a good sparring partner. She got a bloody nose one day, and, ironically enough, that made her even more interested.

Then, Alan began organizing some of the large black tie events in London, for which he is now famous. The lure for Anne was strong. But there was nobody for her to fight. So, she decided to go on a "boxing holiday" to Gleason's Gym in New York. She had made two films in America, and had reason to go over anyway. In late October, 2000, she spent four or five days training on her boxing holiday and finished the experience by having her first fight.

Anne is 126 pounds, and is 5'4" tall. Her greatest fear for this first fight was being knocked out—the "embarrassment factor." She observed that the fight seemed like an eternity, but it was over in an instant, in reality. Her opponent was more experienced. Anne did okay, but she wanted to do better. She went back to the United Kingdom and carried on her training.

Because Adrian Dodson was very busy with his boxing career, she switched trainers to Andy Wallace, a trainer who had almost qualified for the Olympic team, until a benign cyst had been found on his brain. With Andy she had some of the most fantastic training ever. She was training three to four days a week. Her workouts were held in the Lennox Lewis Gym in East London. There are lots of professional boxers there, and it was great for her to see them sparring and training. "All boxers are fantastic people," said Anne. She fought in another charity event with Alan Lacey, and did fine but thought she could have done better. How does she feel about her experiences as a boxer? "I can never take boxing for granted," she says. "There is always a new and exciting challenge."

It is Anne's feeling that white collar boxing has not taken off in the United Kingdom to the same degree as in the United States. This is certainly true for women, and it could be in that regard that Anne made her comment. This could hold true at the amateur level as well. There is no equivalent of the Golden Gloves in Britain, and she is not convinced that the British Boxing Board is totally supportive of women in boxing. Anne feels like the feminine and intellectual nature of the British woman does not lend itself to white collar boxing. She finds her girlfriends more interested in academic pursuits. Further, she commented that she knows many women in London who would "climb a mountain in high heels." She feels that women in white collar boxing are much more accepted in the United States.

Notwithstanding the lack of enthusiasm in England, women have made great strides in white collar boxing in the past few years, particularly in the United States. I am convinced that it will continue to grow in popularity among women, as more and more women discover what a terrific workout it is and how much they can benefit by doing it. The trends are definitely going in the right direction for women, at both the amateur and white collar levels. And if Bert Sugar would take an updated look at some of the matches, I am convinced he would change his attitude toward the quality of the competition that is taking place there today.

I really welcome the rise of women into the sport, and applaud the progress they have made. I followed the careers of my white collar boxing friends, men or women, as best I could, and celebrated their triumphs when I knew about them. As I watch my friends participate in the sport, I realize that over my many years of hard work and competition, I have had as much consistent experience as anyone, save for one. However, there is one man who stands apart from everyone else. His record of accomplishment has certainly surpassed anything I have done, or hope to do. In Thailand, they call him "Farang Ba."

CHAPTER

12

"FARANG BA"

The man who wins may have been counted out several times, but he didn't hear the referee.
—H. E. JANSEN

I first met Craig Wilson at the New York Athletic Club, where he was a member of the NYAC Boxing Team, sometime in the mid-1990s. It was a fairly active time for me on the team, as I was back and forth with the "Turco Wars," as described in chapter 5. However, I always noticed and admired Craig Wilson's boxing style and the way he had of throwing crisp punches. I don't think I ever sparred with him, as I was a heavyweight and he a middleweight. He was balding, an average-looking guy, around 40 at the time: thin, and wore glasses. I learned that he was single.

As I got to know him, I learned that he had quite a pedigree. He was born in Washington, D.C., and graduated from college at Yale, and law school at Harvard. I learned that he was an international corporate attorney, and when we first met, he was at the prestigious international law firm, Coudert

Brothers. He had previously worked at the international law firm, White & Case. I learned that he had a specialization in Southeast Asia, and had previously lived in Bangkok, Thailand, and in the Phillipines. Such a background did not surprise me. I find boxers have incredibly diverse backgrounds. I've met doctors, lawyers, poets, Wall Street professionals, nurses, computer specialists, bankers, taxicab drivers, owners of companies, real estate brokers—every profession you can imagine, and they are usually very successful at whatever they do and fun to be around. Of course, I tend to gravitate toward the financial types. Keep in mind that President Theodore Roosevelt boxed while in the White House.

In late 1997, as I described earlier, I organized a white collar boxing match at Gleason's between the NYAC Boxing Team and Gleason's Gym. Craig Wilson attended this event, and was a very enthusiastic participant. A photograph of all those who fought that evening, including Craig Wilson, hangs in my apartment. He even attended my usual post-fight celebration in Little Italy. In late 1998, Craig left New York to move to Bangkok to join the Coca-Cola Company as an international attorney. At some point, he made a shift to a private equity firm there. Through the film *Farang Ba*, and through our continued contact over the years, I got wind of his most interesting life story.

Craig Wilson began boxing as a white collar middleweight in 1988 at the age of 32, while living in the Phillipines. He got into boxing because his father died from a heart attack caused by being overweight for many years. Craig was only 31 years old at the time, and he decided he needed to develop an exercise routine so that he wouldn't ultimately head down the same path. He had never been particularly athletic, but he went to a gym to get some exercise. It turned out to be a gym which offered boxing, among other sports. He told the people in charge when he arrived that he was a 31-year-old lawyer, and wore glasses. He did not think that boxing was where he belonged. The gym personnel replied that they understood his feelings, but the boxing workout would be good exercise for him; they would not try to make a "boxer" out of him. Craig was game, and he began working out in the boxing ring, eventually working up to light sparring.

His first serious bout took him to an open-air ring in a Manila slum to fight a policeman. He decked his opponent in one round, and he secured his first victory. He continued competing every couple of months and began immersing himself in the sport. He befriended the Filipino national boxing team, even serving as their honorary manager at the Barcelona and Atlanta Olympics.

He returned to the States in 1991 to rejoin White & Case, unaware that the fight of his life was just starting: He was diagnosed with ulcerative colitis, an incurable bowel syndrome which renders the sufferer weak and anemic due to internal bleeding and constant diarrhea. Although he was initially able to manage the disorder, his condition deteriorated after he transferred to Bangkok in 1994. The unpredictability of his bowel movements began to seriously disrupt his life.

"For the four years I had colitis, my ability to do sports decreased over time. The last two years I wasn't able to do anything. How can you do road work when you have to rush to the bathroom 20 times a day?" Then doctors discovered a cancerous tumor and told Craig he'd have to have his colon removed. Languishing in the hospital as he underwent chemotherapy, Craig was certain his boxing days were over. But he was determined to focus his mind on achieving a full recovery.

"I needed a goal to get back in shape, although I wasn't sure I'd be able to do much of anything again. Because boxing seemed so unlikely at that point, my goal was to run a marathon. I set myself two goals: I would run the entire distance, and I wanted to break five hours. I succeeded in both. I crossed the finished line in four hours, 56 minutes, and

22 seconds, having run the entire 26 miles. Even crossing the line, gasping for breath, the thought clicked in my mind, 'If you can run the marathon, you've beaten cancer.' "

But the tumor had left a permanent legacy—he had to be fitted with a colostomy bag. According to Dr. Bruce Orkin, Craig's surgeon, "The major issues these people deal with are body image and the feeling that they're chronically ill because they have a colostomy. This can be devastating to many people." Craig said, "I'm probably the only person, maybe in history, who was relieved to discover he had cancer. I know that sounds really strange, but the colitis was out of control and I had lost hope of ever getting it under control. Having the pouch meant that I no longer had to run to the bathroom every five minutes on a sudden overwhelming urge: I could begin to lead a more normal life again." Wilson returned to training about six months after his operation. "It just felt so good to get back in the ring. I felt as if I'd found a long-lost friend."

Before stepping into the ring, Craig tapes the colostomy bag to his body, and keeps it snug against his skin with cycling shorts and a foul protector designed to protect against low blows. Even so, he concedes: "If I lived in the U.S. and wanted to participate as an amateur boxer, I don't think I would be allowed to at all, given my medical history and the fact that I have a colostomy."

By anyone's analysis, Craig Wilson is no ordinary person. Now in his late forties, he is an avid white collar boxer who steps into the ring at any opportunity and usually does so against opponents half his age. He has fought all over Thailand—in small villages, on Thai army bases, and in the city of Bangkok. Several of his matches have been televised. He continually surprises spectators, not only because he is a "white foreigner," but also because of his age. Each time a match ends and Craig takes off his headgear, there is a wave of shock and amazement as the crowd realizes that they have been actually been watching a balding, middle-aged man who happens to posses the energy and spirit of a twenty-year-old. Craig has been fondly dubbed "Farang Ba," which means "crazy white foreigner" in Thai, by his friends and coaches.

His passion for the sport of amateur boxing has introduced him to a world he would otherwise never have been exposed to. The friendships he had made through boxing are special and unique. Despite Thailand's thriving ex-pat community, most of Craig's friends are native Thai. He is active in his community, helping to sponsor many of the junior national boxing team members. He also served as an Honorary Manager of the Philippine Olympic Boxing Team in Barcelona, Spain in 1992. Ironically, as he approaches 50, Craig Wilson could well be the best international diplomat for the sport of white collar boxing, or even amateur boxing, today. In 2002, Naked Emperor Productions released a one hour documentary film entitled *Farang Ba: Crazy White Foreigner,* which chronicles his story—his background, his fight with cancer and colostomy, his impressive career as an international attorney, and his relentless boxing schedule, which includes one or two competitive matches a month. His trainer, a Thai by the name of Khun Decha, describes Craig: "Craig really makes the effort to work out, to be healthy. He does not fear cancer. He won't give up. He is the perfect athlete."

Craig says in the film: "I love the sport of boxing. I do it because I enjoy it. I do it because it's a challenge every time I go to the gym, every time I climb into the ring. So I do it for fun. I do it for love of the sport. . . . At age 45, competing against guys who are probably half my age, I don't expect to win. I try to win. I want to win. I sure do my best. But to me, success, if you will, is being able to climb in the ring and go at it and do my best. Whether I am the one who wins at the end, or not, ultimately doesn't matter."

To present the depth of Craig's influence and reach within the boxing world in Thailand and around the world of white collar and amateur boxing, I submit the text of an email he sent me in a holiday message in late 2003:

> *Early in the year I met Chai Ratanasuban, the son of Thailand's foremost boxing promoter. Khun Chai saw "Farang Ba: Crazy White Foreigner," the documentary film about me, and borrowed the tape to show to his father. Khun Songchai, bemused by a 47-year-old lawyer who relishes climbing in the ring against opponents half his age, offered me the opportunity of a lifetime: the chance to fight at Sanam Luang, an historic open area near the Grand Palace (roughly akin to the Mall in Washington) that is reserved for royal ceremonies, as part of the traditional, exuberant festivities to mark the King's birthday.*
>
> *To appreciate the honor and the excitement I felt, you must understand the King's role in Thai society. A Thai speaks not of "the King" but of "my King." Every Thai person, from the busiest businessman in Bangkok to the weary woman who peddles delectable roast chicken by the side of the road in Chaiyaphum Province, feels a personal relationship with His Majesty, a relationship that we cynical Americans can scarcely fathom. Imagine that George Washington occupied the White House today, and you will have a sense of the profound love and respect in which all Thais hold this man. By no accident do people refer to his birthday as Father's Day, for he is the national father of every person in the Kingdom.*
>
> *In the evening, tens of thousands of people gather in Sanam Luang at dusk to light candles and sign a special birthday hymn for the King. During the day, the area draws throngs as well for a variety of events, including nationally televised boxing matches. This year, Khun*

Songchai's promotion featured four professional championships. Following the pros, I had my turn to climb in the ring—a first for amateur boxing and a first for a resident foreigner.

Each time I box, win or lose, I feel as though I again confront—and defeat—the cancer that laid me low seven years ago. This time, I felt even more deeply how truly blessed I am. Fortune did not just smile. It grinned.

Before a crowd that easily exceeded 5,000 people, I not only won but—another first—KO'd my 26-year-old opponent in the third round. After he fell to the canvas, the referee motioned me to the neutral corner while he administered the 8-count (a standard safety precaution in amateur boxing). Only, this time, he didn't stop at 8. He got to 10; Khun Pumin still sprawled on the canvas; the ring doctor jumped in to check on him. I returned to my corner, where my coach removed my headgear (prompting then usual "aaahhh" as the crowd realized that I was only young at heart), then went over to check on Khun Pumin. Fortunately, no serious injury, although he admitted to a headache when we went to dinner that evening. The referee then summoned me to the center of the ring and hoisted my hand in victory.

Afterwards, Khun Chai urged me to take a victory walk along the catwalk that surrounded the ring to acknowledge people's cheers. Lots of people held up their hands to touch my gloves and called out to congratulate me; never have I felt more strongly the warmth and friendliness of the Thai people.

I have to admit that the King's Birthday event was a significant highlight. I've never liked KO's—I always like to see a bout go to the end and have a winner declared on points, since I don't want to see injuries. But having said that, I'd be hypocritical if I didn't say that it was pretty cool to see what I was capable of accomplishing.

*Next year's events (although nothing yet scheduled)
will likely include a match with the Thai Team middleweight; a rematch with a Thai paratrooper (I beat him
the first time, he won the second time); a rematch with a
Thai Army light heavyweight (I lost the first time, but,
on reviewing the film, am absolutely convinced that I can
beat him if I'm just more aggressive and take the fight to
him); and a match with the Thai Team B light heavyweight. All of these guys are friends, but they honor me
by not playing when we get in the ring, so it's always a
real fight to the finish.*

Craig Wilson's story is one of tenacity, cross-cultural
respect and courage. He is truly an inspiration to me. Perhaps
his story harkens to the true meaning of sweet science, and its
backdrop in white collar boxing. I salute you, Farang Ba!

CHAPTER

13

THE INCOMPARABLE, UNCONQUERABLE BRUCE LEE

A good fight should be like a small play,
but played seriously. . . . A good martial artist does
not become tense, but ready. Not thinking yet not
dreaming. Ready for whatever may come.
—BRUCE LEE

I can not remember when, exactly, I began to get a clear vision of Bruce Lee. He'd been making his mark on the world since the late 1960s. In those days I was living in Texas for the most part and, though I remember him and might have even seen one of his movies, I paid little attention. Martial arts were in their infancy in this country, and Texas was hardly the place in those days to focus a lot of attention on someone of Asian descent. Also, physical fitness was not a priority for me in the early part of my adult life. Bruce Lee did not reach my radar screen in a meaningful way until a couple of years ago, almost 30 years after his death in 1973.

In 2003, I happened to see a movie that more appropriately introduced me to Bruce Lee. "Dragon: The Bruce Lee Story," is the story of Bruce Lee's life, starring Jason Scott Lee (no relation). I was so moved by it that I bought many of his major films, including *Enter the Dragon, Return of the Dragon, The Chinese Connection, Fists of Fury, The Game of Death,* and *A Warrior's Journey*. I highly recommend all of these movies. I then read several books written by him and about him. His life is an amazing story, a history of the development of martial arts in this country and his rise from nowhere to become one of the biggest movie stars of that era. His philosophy and teachings are even more amazing, and provide penetrating insight into the connection between mind and body and how they must work together to allow someone pursuing any of the martial arts, including boxing, to its highest form of excellence. I feel that Bruce Lee had his pulse on the true meaning of sweet science, even if his perspective was from that of a martial artist, as opposed to a traditional boxer.

Fred Weintraub, co-producer of *Enter the Dragon*, the very successful martial arts movie that made Bruce Lee famous, observed, "There's an incomparable beauty that's like a deadly kind of ballet to the martial arts. Regardless of the hostility in them, one can't deny the thrill of watching a great fighter go through his paces." Weintraub undoubtedly said this with the great Bruce Lee, a martial arts perfectionist, in mind. Other images of Bruce Lee were advanced by John Little, when he referred to him in a book by the same name as an "artist of life." Little described Bruce Lee as "the poet, the philosopher, the psychologist, the man of letters, the motivator, the self-help advocate, the artist, the actor, the sociologist, the soulsearcher." This is a lot more than what usually comes to mind when you think of a martial artist. And in being all of these things, Bruce Lee knew that it is only in the process of coming to know ourselves that we can come to know anything. I have found this concept of self-knowledge to be a very important one in white collar boxing, and in other things I have accomplished in my life. Knowing myself means to know both my strengths and limitations. At the same time, I am able to continually challenge myself to be the best that I can be, but do so in a smart and skillful way.

Although Bruce Lee was reared in Hong Kong, he was born in San Francisco on November 27, 1940, the Chinese Year of the Dragon. The dragon is considered the most powerful—and most benevolent—creature in Chinese mythology. When Bruce was born, his father, Hoi Chuen Lee, an opera singer, was traveling on the East Coast of the United States. Grace Lee, his mother, had remained on the West Coast in anticipation of the arrival of her fourth child, Bruce. After five months, Bruce and his parents returned to Hong Kong. Politically, socially, and economically diverse, Hong Kong has been for many years the Asian equivalent of Manhattan. Everywhere there was a feeling of crowds, of being swept along on a surging wave of human activity. Hong Kong in the 1950s was a place suffering from high unemployment, a depressed economy, overcrowding, homelessness—and from people simply taking advantage of each other due to these difficult circumstances. Bruce developed a combative reputation at an early age, and was transferred from one parochial school to another because of his constant fighting, even though his teachers seemed to like him, according to Grace Lee. Long after Bruce had left school for the U.S., he was still remembered as a bully and troublemaker.

To Bruce, Hong Kong seemed to be a city of ghettos, of the economically deprived, where everyone was struggling to make ends meet, but coming up short. Under these conditions, it was natural for a young man to want to belong to a gang. Bruce confided, "I took up kung fu . . . when I began to feel insecure. I kept wondering what would happen to me if my gang was not around when I met a rival gang." Actually, Bruce, who was Cantonese, preferred to pronounce his art as "gung fu" instead of "kung fu," although I will refer to it as kung fu, as this name had been popularized in

America by a television series of that name which was originated in the 1970s.

Kung fu is an ancient Chinese fighting art, an ancestor of karate and jujitsu, but more fluid with continuity of movement. Actually, there are several variations of kung fu: the kind Bruce Lee practiced was wing chun. From time to time in his early days in Hong Kong, matches between rival gangs would take place, frequently on roofs of tall buildings. Usually, the combatants were students from two different styles of kung fu, battling to determine which was the superior style. In his later adolescent years, he continued to practice forms of kung fu, and began to work on his efforts to develop his flowing energy. Martial artists usually refer to this inner energy as *ch'i*— variously translated as spirit or life-force.

Without any boxing training, Bruce entered an amateur boxing contest his senior year in high school, and was declared Hong Kong High School Champion. He left Hong Kong for the United States in 1959, and found here a country virtually devoid of the traditional martial arts; there were only forms of judo and jujitsu, two Japanese arts that were taught to U.S. servicemen in the Korean War. The term martial arts applies to a wide variety of highly combative fighting methods, such as karate, jujitsu, Chinese kung fu or Chinese boxing, tae kwon do, and others. Bruce continued the study of kung fu. He was an innovator and very creative. He would constantly find ways to increase his power and speed in fighting. Only 5'7" in height, Bruce became 135 pounds of martial arts dynamite.

Bruce was a student of boxing, and had hundreds of boxing manuals and dozens of films, which he would watch and analyze with his friends. He collected films of many great boxers, including Joe Louis, Rocky Marciano, Jack Dempsey, Max Baer, and Muhammad Ali. Bruce's boxing idol was Muhammad Ali, who he felt was the greatest heavyweight boxer he had ever seen. Bruce watched Ali's films over and over again until he knew most of his movements. However, to adapt his techniques he would watch them through a reflection in a mirror, as Bruce was a lefty, and Ali's image would come through in the mirror's reflection as a "south-paw." "Growing up in the sixties and seventies, I thought of myself as following the 'way' (the Tao) of Ali," Bruce Lee was later to say. He even tried Thai boxing and *savate* (French footfighting).

It is an interesting exercise to compare boxing to the martial arts, and I cannot adequately analyze them in just these few paragraphs. Nevertheless, a few general statements can be made. First, the history of the martial arts emanates from the Orient. Boxing, as we have already mentioned, has more comprehensive geographic origins.

The sports themselves have both similarities and differences. Like boxing, most martial arts are combative styles based on attack. A notable exception to this is judo, which Chris Angle describes as a more defensive sport. He calls it "wrestling with clothes on," where you defend yourself first. Further, he states that in judo, each fighter tries to use the opponent's own inertia against him. In judo, leverage is applied so that an opponent can eventually be taken down.

Boxing, on the other hand, is a ferocious, true warrior sport, similar to gladiatorial combat where the fighters must face each other head-on. However, the rules are more defined in boxing. For instance, kicking is not allowed in boxing whereas kicking is an integral part of most martial arts.

Personally, I have always had great respect for the martial arts, and wanted to study them in greater depth. There has always been something very mysterious about them, shrouded in cultural tradition, mental discipline, and combative excellence. For me, Bruce Lee was an important connection to the martial arts. As I continued my study of Bruce Lee, I was looking for ways to connect white collar boxing to his teachings, and apply them to bring my skills to a higher level.

Bruce attended the University of Washington, where he majored in philosophy. He had only a year left when he left for Oakland. Though he wasn't a particularly good student, he was erudite in Oriental philosophy (Taoism, Zen, etc.). His study of philosophy had a great influence on his approach to the martial arts and to the way he lived his life. His definition of philosophy was the Western ethos version meaning "the love of wisdom." He became a brilliant philosopher about everyday living, and this was exemplified in his pursuit of the martial arts. He felt that the mark of a good human being was one who honestly knew himself or herself. The martial arts helped him to achieve this goal, and to honestly express himself. At the core of his beliefs was that all types of knowledge ultimately led to self-knowledge, which was his goal. It was constantly striving to achieve this goal that would allow him to reach perfection in the martial arts.

His approach to the martial arts was all about personal growth. Until he decided to devote himself to acting full-time, he taught the martial arts to others. However, he did not view himself as a "teacher," per se, but as one who could help others explore themselves. He felt that "a teacher, a really good *sensei* (instructor or master), is never a *giver* of 'truth,' he is a guide, a pioneer to the truth that the student must discover for himself."

Bruce was a health enthusiast, but probably should not be described as an extremist. He drank milk instead of coffee. He avoided cigarettes and alcoholic beverages, but never refused a cup of hot tea. However, he would eat anything: fish, chicken, beef, pork, and vegetables. He was particularly partial to Chinese and Japanese fare. He had a voracious appetite, often ordering a second plate of food in a restaurant. He also drank a lot of water, and took a daily amount of vitamin pills, apparently influenced by a bodybuilding magazine which he received in the mail periodically. He prided himself in being so healthy. He used to say, "I want to be the healthiest and strongest 50-year-old man alive." But fate would not allow him to achieve this goal.

Bruce Lee trained hard. He referred to running as the "king of all exercises," and he ran daily, usually a four-mile, 24-minute run. He believed that sit-ups and leg raises were a must for a martial artist to be in condition. Stretching was a very important part of his workout. He did not believe a fighter needed big, bulky muscles, but that the body should be muscular and supple. He felt that being supple also helped his motion. By being supple, he felt that his body moved more smoothly, more fluidly. As a result of his training regimen, Bruce moved with the finesse of a ballet dancer. He worked out with weights, but he also worked out with other equipment such as a trampoline, and several different types of punching bags. He would do endless chin-ups. He made up his own exercises to achieve his goals, and created several apparatuses to assist him to exercise. He even fashioned his weight training exercise to avoid bulky muscles that might interfere with his performance. Yet, his muscles were like pure steel.

He followed a daily ritual. Since he didn't hold a steady job, he took the necessary time to exercise, as he considered exercise and training his full-time job. This usually consisted of performing his four-mile run on hilly terrain, working out with weights, and kicking and punching a dummy apparatus built by himself and his students. He concentrated on his abdominal muscles because he believed that the body is the biggest target and the least mobile. He believed that more muscles you have around your abdomen, the more blows it can take. He would do his sit-ups very slowly, his body descending slower than ascending. He felt that he received more benefit by doing them slowly, as his body received more resistance. Similarly, he did not emphasize the number of repetitions but the way they were done.

Everything Bruce indulged in had to be almost perfect. For instance, he would spend hours doing a rapid side kick until his motion was smooth and almost a blur. He would train until a particular movement he was striving to achieve was perfect.

All of this led him to the development of his own style of martial arts, which he called *jeet kune do,* or "the way of the intercepting fist." Most martial arts are styles based on attack. Jeet kune do is based on the principal of *interception.* I have translated this term into its simplest interpretation, defensive fighting, which I have absolutely come to believe in. Bruce's jeet kune do is much more complicated and scientific than the sole concept of defense, however.

Bruce Lee resisted the concept of referring to jeet kune do as a style, per se. Rather than having a set style, or set reaction, to a given set of circumstances in self defense, Bruce's jeet kune do favors a more free form of movement. A precise definition is not easy. Unlike a "classical" martial art, there is no series of rules or classification of technique that constitutes a distinct jeet kune do method of fighting.

Let me start to define it by saying what jeet kune do is not—it is not rigid, but is free form; it is not a set of special movements with its own set philosophy; it does not approach combat from a single point of view, but from all angles; it is not bound by any rules or restrictions, and is therefore free to react to any style or situation. It is based on reacting to movement and countering motion and force by intercepting the motion or force, whatever it might be. It is also based on efficiency of motion—rather than going through a set pattern of movement and wasted motion, someone efficient in jeet kune do will, in effect, counter attack any movement with strength and speed. It is not based on repeating imitative drills as conditioned responses. Rather, jeet kune do favors formlessness, so that the fighter can assume all forms and react to the situation at hand.

It was in the teachings of Jiddu Krishnamurti, in particular, that Bruce Lee found the philosophical framework of jeet

kune do. Jiddu Krishnamurti was born in 1895 to an impover-
ished family in Southern India. His spirituality was recognized
at an early age, and he spoke and lectured throughout his life
that organized religions and sects stood in the way of the truth.
Krishnamurti did not deny traditional approaches to self-
realization, but he also left himself open to others. Bruce Lee
took many of Krishnamurti's beliefs and applied them to his
own philosophies, including his approach to self-realization
and the martial arts. In applying Krishnamurti's principles to
the martial arts, Bruce Lee believed there is not just one
response to a given situation in combat—a fighter should be
free to respond in many ways.

Bruce Lee, in his own poetic way, likened a description of
jeet kune do to water—yes, the simplest substance we all
know, plain water. Below is a synopsis of his thinking on
water, and in reading it, one should imagine its application to
fighting and the martial arts:

"See how it flows
Be like water
Water's the softest stuff in the world
But it can fit into any container"

"Water . . . is insubstantial
. . . You can not grasp hold of it
You can not punch or hurt it"

"It seems weak
But it can penetrate rock
Be like the nature of water"

"Please observe the adaptability of water
If you squeeze it fast,
The water will flow out quickly
If you squeeze it slowly,

It will come out slowly
Water may seem to move in contradiction, even uphill,
But it chooses any way open to it so that it may reach the sea
It may flow swiftly or it may flow slowly,
But its purpose is inexorable, its destiny sure"

"Water is so fine that it is impossible to grasp a handful of it
Strike it, yet is does not suffer hurt,
Stab it, and it is not wounded
Sever it, yet it is not divided
It has not shape of its own,
But molds itself to the receptacle that contains it
When heated to the state of steam it is invisible
But has enough power to split the earth itself
When frozen it crystallizes into a mighty rock
First it is turbulent like Niagra Falls,
And then calm like a still pond, fearful like a torrent,
And refreshing like a hot summer's day"

"If you try to remember, you will lose
Empty your mind
Be formless, shapeless
Like water
Now, you put water into a cup, it becomes the cup
You put water into a bottle, it becomes the bottle
You put (water) in a teapot, it becomes the teapot
Now water can flow, or creep, or drip, or it can crash
Be water, my friend"

"Running water never grows stale
So you've just got to keep on flowing"

Through Bruce Lee, I began to realize what a truly amazing substance that water is. To go back further in history, principles regarding water were applied to war and the movement of armies in Sun-Tzu's *The Art of War* as early as the early Chou Dynasty in ancient China (1045–256 B.C.), where it was noted that water has no constant shape, and one is able to wrest victory by being able to change and transform in accord with the enemy. However, Bruce Lee successfully applied these principles more directly to hand-to-hand combat and the martial arts.

In fairness, these principles of water are also based on the teachings of kung fu, or more particularly, the *Tao* of kung fu. "Kung fu is a special kind of skill, a fine art rather than just a physical exercise or self defense. To the Chinese, kung fu is the subtle art of matching the essence of the mind to that of the techniques in which it has to work. The principle of kung fu . . . has to grow spontaneously, like a flower, in a mind free from desires and emotions. The core of this principle of kung fu is Tao—the spontaneity of the universe."

The word *Tao* has no exact equivalent in the English language. In *Masterpieces of World Philosophy*, "Tao, the way, is the nameless beginning of things, the universal principle underlying everything, the supreme, ultimate pattern, and the principle of growth." Stated in layman's language, even though there is no specific word for Tao, its meaning has often been interpreted as "truth" or "way." Therefore, the Tao of kung fu can be thought of as the truth or way of kung fu.

Tao operates in yin-yang, a pair of mutually complementary forces that are at work in and behind all phenomena. This principle of yin-yang, also known as *T'ai Chi,* is the basic structure of kung fu. They are opposite principles—yang is whiteness, positiveness, and masculinity; yin is blackness, negativeness, and femininity. Yang is day and yin is night. Yang is heat and yin is coldness, and so forth. In reality, they are mutually interdependent with cooperation and alternation. The principles of yin-yang in kung fu are expressed as the *Law of Harmony*, and both are essential to the universe. It states that one should be in harmony with, not in rebellion against, the strength and force of the opposition. As Bruce Lee studied this, he came to realize that one of the fundamental applications of this was achievement of a state of harmony for a fighter was the ability to relax and to react to what was before him in combat. In this way, the fighter achieves harmony within himself.

"Relax" is a word which is thrown around a lot in modern-day boxing at all levels. You might not understand its application fully until you've had a lot of experience in the ring. However, I believe that it is these principles of kung fu that are the root of the true meaning of "relax" in the boxing ring today. Bruce Lee's only real martial arts instructor, Professor Yip Man, head of the wing chun school of kung fu, would tell Bruce to relax and calm his mind, to forget about himself and follow the opponent's movement. The Professor advanced another concept to him, the art of *detachment*, which means to counter any aggressive movements an opponent makes, without undue deliberation. This, in its essence, means to fight in a relaxed state, reacting simultaneously to what you find in the ring before you, an extremely important concept in boxing.

With these concepts in mind, Bruce Lee felt that any set of rigid rules in combat would be less efficient and successful than someone who could operate with a more free-form approach. He felt that anyone trying to remember rules would ultimately not be successful in a real combat situation.

As I continued to read and study Bruce Lee's philosophy on the martial arts and fighting, its truth began to sink in. His teachings, combined with my readings of kung fu and jeet kune do, affected me profoundly. I realized that my approach to boxing at that time was the antithesis of free form. I operated by a rigid set of rules. I even had a checklist of about 20 movements I used in a fight, which I always took with me to each fight. I read them and studied them the day of each fight, and read them over and over in the locker room right before each fight. The television special done by MSNBC made a big deal about this, and actually showed me in front of my computer going over these rules, and later before the fight in my dressing room reviewing them again and again. Here is a partial list of the things I was attempting to remember:

- Jab continuously
- Ring movement
- Side to side, but jab when I am doing this
- Hands up, particularly the right when I jab
- Don't drop the hand I am not punching with
- Defense—don't let him touch me
- Straight punches
- Extend punches
- If cornered, short punches
- Keep chin down
- Keep hands up, elbows in
- Don't clinch—push off or punch out of it
- Breathe
- Move laterally
- Use my size to my advantage
- Fake
- Control
- Exhale when punching
- Relax
- NO FAVORS

I had begun to count on this list—it was like a security blanket. However, I realized that Bruce Lee was right—my rehearsed routines meant that I could not always adapt to a given situation in the ring. I realized that I had to direct my boxing from my own heart, rather than just emulating someone else, or operating from a set playbook of rules. I began to approach fighting in a different manner. In short, I began to apply the principles of Bruce Lee's philosophy of the martial arts and jeet kune do to my boxing. I had been fighting by a set of rules, not from my soul. I was determined to change.

To complete the story of Bruce Lee, he found his way into the movies. But this had a purpose in his life, as did everything he did. He used the motion picture industry to show his way of living the martial arts, and the unique power and beauty of the Asian culture. He showed the world that it was not size and strength that matters, but focus. He was a complete perfectionist, hand drawing each scene in a movie in great detail before it was filmed. His fight scenes had to be absolutely perfect, no matter the number of takes required to achieve his desired perfection. The resulting movies were truly works of art. His movies, books, teachings, and writings carry a message as powerful today as when he was alive, over 30 years ago. What a tragedy that he lived such a short life of only 32 years. The circumstances surrounding his death on July 20, 1973, remain shrouded in mystery, although some sources report he died from complications directly related to his martial arts. Others link his death to an adverse reaction to a prescription drug.

Regardless, he was a man who frequently in his life looked directly into the abyss, and it consumed him in the end. From the beginning, he pushed himself beyond all reasonable physical and mental limits. Throughout his life, he was apparently haunted by unexplainable dreams and nightmares. Part of this could have been his own insecurities and self-doubts manifesting themselves in the form of dreams. In any case, what matters most to us today is the exemplary way he lived, the lives he touched, the writings and movies he left behind, the family and friends he loved and who loved him, the teachings he gave to his students, and the high standards of excellence he imposed on the martial arts and on everything he did. His funeral in Hong Kong five days after his death was attended by 25,000 people, the largest in the city's history. He is buried in Seattle.

His principles and teachings definitely help refine the meaning of the sweet science of boxing, for those who have studied his works. According to legendary folksinger Phil Ochs, in describing the martial arts expertise of Bruce Lee, "It is not the vulgarity of James Arness, pistol-whipping a drunken stage robber (from the television series *Gunsmoke*). . . . It is not the ingenious devices of James Bond coming to the rescue, nor the ham-fisted John Wayne slugging it out in the saloon over crumbling tables and paper-thin imitation glass. It is the science of the body taken to its highest form, and the violence, no matter how outrageous, is always strangely purifying."

Through Bruce Lee, I was able to take my boxing to the next level. While I would hesitate to say that I "threw away the book," I was able to use what I learned from him in a most positive way, and supplement my existing methods with his principles and teachings. And I was to prove it, later that year against a big, strong collegiate boxer about one-third my age.

CHAPTER

14

TASTING THE
SWEET SCIENCE

That feeling in your heart supersedes anything.
—SERGIO MORA FROM *THE CONTENDER* TELEVISION SHOW

In early 2003, Dan O'Leary, Mike Fullam, and Emory Borhi, the boxing coaches of the New York Athletic Club, announced a fight night with the Trinity Gym for early November. It was to be held at the Trinity Gym, which is in the Wall Street area. The original date set for this was November 6. Dan and Emory were eager to step up the boxing program at the NYAC, and approached me to see if Bruce Silverglade at Gleason's would be interested in having us there sometime also. I called Bruce, and he was very interested in having our team come to Gleason's for one of his white collar shows. We settled on the date at Gleason's for November 21, 2003, a Friday night, as always. However, schedules in boxing are frequently changed, and the Trinity show was moved to Thursday, November 20. So our team now had two boxing dates, back to back, November 20 at the Trinity and November 21 at Gleason's.

As a boxer, one thing you do not want to have is boxing

matches back to back on successive nights—it is simply too difficult a task, both mentally and physically. So our team members got to choose which of the dates they preferred. Of the eight or nine guys participating, about half chose the Trinity and the other half chose Gleason's. Since I had been instrumental in setting up the Gleason's show, I elected that one. Also, my company's holiday party was the night of the Trinity show.

By the time of the fights, however, most of our team members had shifted over to the Trinity show for one reason or another. I could not do this because of my company's holiday party. So I was the lone representative of the NYAC boxing team at Gleason's the night of November 21, 2003. It did not matter. I was right where I wanted to be, mentally and physically.

Following my sparring session with Senator Bruno on October 22, I was in great shape physically. I had just returned from Gleason's Boxing Camp the weekend before, where I had worked out rigorously, and had enjoyed a good bout with Pat O'Lear. I truly felt I was at the top of my game. Over the course of the summer, I had been introduced to the teachings of Bruce Lee. I took a few of his books to the Gleason's Boxing Camp, and read them in the off hours. I had a great time training at the Gleason's Boxing Camp with Juan Laporte, Mark Breland, Matthew Said Muhammad, Carlos Ortiz, and Emile Griffith, all former world champions. The match with the senator was exciting and a good workout— even a bit glamorous with the press coverage and the other senators in attendance. As the late fall approached, I was in good spirits and fit. When the Trinity and Gleason's matches were announced by the NYAC Boxing Team coaches, I was ready.

In late October and through November, as I trained for the Gleason's match, I continued reading and studying the teachings of Bruce Lee. I watched as many of his movies as I could find. I became transfixed by his teachings and philosophy. I expanded beyond his teachings of jeet kune do to the Tao of kung fu. I was particularly impressed with the concept of water and its free form. The concept of formlessness and shapelessness was something I had never thought about before. This helped me truly relax in the ring, and began to allow me to better follow the movements of my sparring partners and react to their aggressions. I sought to harmonize with the movements of my sparring partners.

The translation which Bruce Lee gave to jeet kune do was "the way of the intercepting fist." Accordingly, by relaxing and allowing oneself to simply react to aggression, rather than approaching an opponent with a canned, pre-programmed set of moves, a boxer can glide through a boxing workout in a much more free-form manner. This is the essence of what my trainer, Ricky Young, would call *defense*.

At this stage of my career, my idea of a good fight is one in which my opponent does not lay a glove on me. I do not like being hit, particularly in the face. I don't think being hit in the face is a good for anyone, despite all the macho talk around boxing and other martial arts. I have always avoided it by fighting very defensively—keeping my hands in front of my face, using lots of ring movement, circling, and head and body movement. Ricky Young has preached this to me for years. "Defense, defense, defense," he would scream at me. I know that in real estate, the old cliché is "location, location, location." "Defense, defense, defense" works the same way in boxing, and is the key to success in the ring, at least for me.

I called Ricky Young when I heard about the upcoming night at Gleason's. We began the regimen of preparing for a fight. As described earlier, training is a seven-day-a-week proposition leading up to a fight. Sometimes I would work out twice a day, so I could have as many as ten or eleven workouts in a week. The workouts would be a combination of sparring, boxing gym work (like jump rope, bag work, shadow boxing, mitts, and push-ups/sit-ups), weights, and running.

I would frequently rise at 5 A.M., and run three to four miles. I would then work a full day, arriving in the office by 7 A.M. After a full day, I might spar or do weights. It was a grind. However, when the Trinity and Gleason's matches were announced by the NYAC coaches in late October, I was already in good shape. With less than one month to go, I accelerated my training with the confidence that I could now take myself to a higher level than ever before, if I were to dig down and make it happen.

As I trained, I kept the concept of Bruce Lee's interpretation of water at the forefront of my mind. I was blown away by this concept. I wanted to apply it to my boxing. I told Ricky Young about it, and he was equally impressed with the possibility of this advancement in my boxing career. I told him I wanted this fight to be more free form. I wanted to counter attack any movement with strength and speed. I wanted to truly relax in the ring and fight without set conditioned responses. I wanted to fight spontaneously, in an unprogrammed way. Through this, I hoped to learn more about myself and my abilities. I hoped to learn the *Tao* of John Oden.

In many ways, this was a risk, but at what cost? It was not like I was going to ever make a living as a boxer. George Foreman I was not. I was way past the age of an Olympic boxer. So why not challenge myself in this way, to see if I could really make some significant improvements in my game? The only real risk was the risk of getting hurt. In some ways, having a style and a repetitive set of moves to rely upon, which had worked for me in the past, offered a sense of comfort and security. There were certain things I knew I could count on—my jab, my big right hand. They were like old friends and protectors. There was a comfort zone, which gave a great sense of security. Could I do things differently? Could I do so without getting hurt?

As I pondered this, I recalled an experience that I had two or three years previously when sparring with Chris Angle, my traditional sparring partner at the NYAC, with whom I have probably sparred 1,000 rounds over the ten years we have been swinging at each other. One day, without warning to Chris, at the urging of Jack Kendrick, I switched from a right-hander to a left-hander. Chris Angle is an extremely good boxer, who probably is a kindred spirit to Bruce Lee. He is very fluid in his movements, and can spar with anyone, despite weight, experience, or age. He is a reactive counter puncher, not a big slugger, but a great defensive fighter. He is a great sparring partner and has become one of my closest friends over the ten or so years we have sparred together.

Chris Angle was not even surprised by this new move. Within seconds, he hit me with several hard shots, and I quickly switched back to my right-hand style. At that point in my career, this was my one and only experience at trying something really new. And I got clocked!

Despite this, I resolved to apply some of the principles I had learned and read from the teachings of Bruce Lee to my own boxing style. I memorized the passages which Bruce Lee had written about water. I watched his movies over and over. I studied his teachings and his writings. I learned more and more.

Ricky was impressed with my efforts, and encouraged me to continue to pursue this. In sparring sessions, I became more fluid, more spontaneous. Surprisingly, I retained a lot of things I had learned, but supplemented them with these thoughts of relaxation, harmony, and formlessness. I worked on counterattacking any movement towards me with strength and speed. As the training went on, I felt myself getting stronger. Chris Angle told me that he felt I was as good as I had ever been. I was handling him better, feeling stronger, more confident. As always, confidence in the ring brought its rewards to me in my daily activities. I felt extremely fit and agile. I lost weight and gained confidence. My clothes began to fit loosely. My work was going well. All of this translated to terrific personal growth, which is the ultimate goal of athletics. Things were going well for me as November 21 approached.

One of the great uncertainties of a white collar sparring match at Gleason's is the opponent you are to face. This is somewhat different from a club championship at the NYAC, where you are fighting teammates for the club champion title. The uncertainty of facing someone you don't know causes great anxiety in boxing, because as the old cliché goes, "styles make boxing." What this means is that boxing styles can make a big difference in the outcome of a fight. Why did Muhammad Ali have such a tough time with Ken Norton both times they fought? Because Ali had trouble with Norton's very unique style. Why was George Foreman able to destroy Joe Frazier, but lost to Muhammad Ali? Again, styles really matter. That is why the Bruce Lee principles of form-lessness and shapelessness, if they can be implemented by a boxer, are so important. The anxiety of facing a person you have never seen before by squaring off against them in the ring is an extremely daunting experience.

I love being a heavyweight. I think it is the most interesting, the most exciting weight class of all. As a heavyweight, though, I am supposed to fight other heavyweights—if they are at a comparable skill level. The only problem is that heavyweights can be (and usually are) big, ugly guys. Somehow when they have all the gear, the mouthpiece, the headgear, and the big gloves, they look even bigger and uglier. Seeing someone come at you, swinging for your head and meaning it, can be fright-ening even to a seasoned boxer.

So, as the fight approached, I asked Bruce Silverglade if he had anyone in mind for me. He stated that he could think of no one off the top of his head, but fighters always came to the show at the last minute. This is actually true, as boxers come from all over the country to box in a Gleason's show. I would not want to be Bruce Silverglade in making these matchups, but he always seems to do a great job, and the Gleason's shows are always run with the thought of protecting the fighter, first and foremost. I was not worried, just anxious, as always.

As we got closer to the fight, Ricky Young tried out an idea on me. Ricky was coach of the Columbia University Boxing Team, and worked with many students at Columbia. In addition to his duties with the boxing team, he taught several classes on boxing and physical fitness at Columbia. Ricky said he was impressed with a young heavyweight at Columbia, by the name of David Berman. David was a relatively new fighter, but one who was making good progress. Ricky told me three things about David that he'd observed—he was bigger (6'5" as opposed to my 6'4"), younger (19 years old, closer to a third my age than half of it), and physically stronger (Ricky's personal opinion). Just what you want in an opponent! Nevertheless, Ricky thought he might be a good match for me, and me for him, so we began to talk about it. In some ways, I suppose I took some comfort in that Ricky knew us both—knew our strengths, weaknesses, and basic skill levels. I suggested that Ricky speak to David about it. David jumped at the chance! Ricky met with Bruce Silverglade, and the match was made. Now to test my newfound skills. As there were still two weeks to go before the fight, I really went at it.

On Friday, November 21, I had a busy day. My company had a client conference that day which began in the morning and lasted through lunch. Usually, I take off the day of a fight, but not that day. I was not able to leave work until about 4:30. I was not able to do the normal mental preparation and relaxation that I was accustomed to the day of the fight. I arrived at Gleason's around 6:30. The fights were slated to begin at 7:30, but always ran late, sometimes as late as 8 o'clock.

Neither Ricky nor David Berman were there. In fact, they did not show up until around 7:15. Ricky brought David to the gym, because David had never been to Gleason's before. He was huge! Later I learned that he was an undergraduate student studying math at Columbia. He looked extremely fit.

I was glad I got a glimpse of him before we got in the ring. At least I had time to adjust mentally to the way he looked, which was very impressive.

When David and I entered the ring, we did the normal loosening up exercises, and then Bruce introduced us. I was extremely proud when he announced that this would be an "exciting fight." He introduced me as a "great friend of Gleason's Gym." I got a huge applause. I had invited my entire team from the office; in addition, a number of other friends had shown up, including a few people from the NYAC. Glen Mercante, son of Arthur Mercante, Sr., the former world famous boxing referee, was there. The pressure was on. Interestingly enough, I was not my normal, anxious self. I seemed to be floating; I was truly relaxed. Could it be that Bruce Lee's teachings were working?

The first round started and he came right for me. Reacting to his move to me, I countered him with a hard right, then another one. Ricky Young told me later that he was concerned because I hit him so hard. From that moment on, I seemed to float through the fight. He literally did not lay a glove on me. I worked on everything. I was moving, reacting, trying to be shapeless, formless, elusive, harmonizing. It was working. It felt great, and I know I looked good. David did a fine job, although I am sure it may have frustrated him a little. Other than the first round, I didn't hit him with any really hard shots, but I was truly at the top of my game, and he couldn't find me to inflict any damage whatsoever. When the final bell rang, we hugged each other, as is the gentlemanly custom.

I was very proud of my accomplishment that night. I feel I had truly moved my boxing career forward, for the first time in a long time. Ricky Young summed it up when he said, "John, you fought like a cat tonight." I wish Bruce Lee was alive so I could shake his hand. I finally tasted the sweet science that night, and it was delicious.

It was a great experience for David Berman, as well. After the fight that night, I spent some time with him, and really liked him. I told him I thought he had done a great job. The next day, he wrote an email to me:

> *Dear John,*
>
> *I just wanted to thank you for the excellent experience I had boxing. I learned quite a bit and had a great time. Thanks again for everything, and if you remember, let me know next time you have a fight and I'd love to come and support.*
>
> *David Berman*

I took all my friends in a big limo to my favorite after-fight restaurant, Angelo's on Mulberry Street. The waiters who have seen me there so many times after fights greeted me with open arms. No menus were needed. We dined like royalty and celebrated till the wee hours.

CHAPTER 15

IN MY CORNER

The characters who hold the book, and
the whole fabric of the Sweet Science together,
are the trainer-seconds, as in Egan's day.
—A.J. LIEBLING, *THE SWEET SCIENCE*, 1958

I have read many, many books on boxing. Most of them feature stories about great fights or great fighters. Some talk about the grand history of boxing. Many have been written about boxing in the twentieth century, some of the unforgettable fights that occurred during that period, and some of the legendary fight promoters, like Don King and Bob Arum. Others talk about outstanding referees, like Arthur Mercante, Sr., and Mills Lane.

In all of these writings, the most overlooked man (and I think all are men, none women that I have personally seen) is the corner man or trainer. To my way of thinking, the corner man is the key to the story. He is the most important element in what makes a boxer achieve his potential. He can motivate, inspire, push the fighter hard, and help him continue to challenge himself or herself. This is true at all levels of boxing—professional, amateur, and white collar.

The work of a corner man or trainer begins long before an actual fight. I have made a point of trying to stay in "okay" shape by "maintaining" at all times, as described earlier. All of my boxing workouts are accompanied by a trainer, who is also almost always in my corner for the fight.

But when I am training for a fight, it is another story. As I mentioned, I frequently train seven days a week, sometimes two times a day, and usually three of these workouts are boxing workouts. My trainer is with me for these boxing workouts, and we speak on the phone constantly in between training sessions. During the course of this regimen, a boxer gets to know his trainer quite well. The trainer is constantly giving feedback and advice on how the boxer is doing. He is the person holding the mitts, and the person giving instruction during sparring sessions.

It is also the trainer who helps the fighter with questions on training regimen, diet, hours of sleep, and anything else that comes up as the fighter goes about preparing for a fight. The trainer is the one person a boxer can talk to, confide in, and share his frustrations with, both inside the ring and out. The trainer is more than an instructor; he is a friend, counselor, and even a psychiatrist of sorts.

Most important, during those lonely moments in the ring, when no one else is there, the corner man can be a fighter's salvation. It's hard to describe to someone who has never boxed how important this can be. As the fight time approaches, the trainer not only becomes the boxer's close friend, he becomes his best friend. On fight night, he becomes his only friend.

Above all, the trainer is the fighter's "strategic advisor," and to do that, the trainer must know the fight game very well. In practical terms, trainers oversee a fighter's physical preparation for a fight, which will include roadwork, weight training, sparring, weights, rest, and diet. And the trainer will make sure a fighter "makes weight"—weighs no more than the maximum weight allowed for the weight class the fighter is in. He will analyze the strengths and weaknesses of the opponent, and create a strategy for victory. He will warm up the fighter on fight night, escort him to the ring, and be with him at all times leading up to fight time. Then he will advise him in the corner between rounds and help the fighter make the necessary adjustments to his game plan. When necessary, the trainer must know when to stop a fight before his fighter is seriously injured.

But there's more to it than that. Working with a boxer, trainers perform a variety of roles including doctor, psychologist, father figure, babysitter, confidant, motivator, and actor, among others. An article on Teddy Atlas written by David Remnick and published in *The New Yorker*, gives a very poignant look at the relationship of a boxer and a trainer. It describes Teddy Atlas training a young light heavyweight, Elvir Muriqi.

> *Between rounds, Atlas gave his fighter water, as if to a baby; there was great solicitude in the way he held up the bottle with one hand and kept a finger under Muriqi's lip, to prevent dribbling. This kind of physical intimacy, this babying, is unique to boxing. Bill Parcells does not water his fullback; Joe Torre does not massage the pitcher.*

Craig Wilson said in the film *Farang Ba* about his trainer, Decha Boonkamnerd:

> *The relationship between a boxer and a coach is something I find hard to describe to people who haven't experienced it and don't understand it. But it is a tremendously important and close and dependent relationship.*
>
> *Khun Decha is someone on whom I rely absolutely, implicitly, in whose judgment I have complete confidence—*

whether it is during the fight, training for a fight, or after a fight. If I've lost, he says to me—"you tried, you did your best, don't worry about it." If I've done well, he helps me celebrate. If he thinks I've done a good job whether I've won or lost, just a quick look or a quick smile absolutely makes me feel as though I am on top of the world.

Khun Decha says of Craig:

On a coaching level, I have trained him as best I can. I have never doubted his ability and I have passed on whatever I have learned to him. On a personal level, Khun Craig is a very warm and open person. I am not just his coach. I am not just his friend. It's like we are family.

The two trainers who I have worked with the most and the longest, Jack Kendrick and Ricky Young, have both had a huge influence on my life. Both of these men are very engaging personalities, and both are tremendous motivators. Jack Kendrick has a way with words—he's a poet and speaks from the heart. He is a world class athlete, having competed and taught boxing and track and field all over the world. For that reason, I have always called him the poet/warrior, although his boxing handle is "The Dancing Ghost."

The letters that Jack Kendrick wrote to me before some of my biggest fights are among my most cherished possessions. His handwritten words to me before the rubber match with John Turco on October 23, 1996 will always be with me:

You are one of the few who go into the furnace of competition and for that you are a rare, and fortunate, human being. Therefore, whether the outcome be victory or defeat, you have already won.

And then in June 2001, before my fight with Lee Victory in London (even though he could not attend), his concluding remarks in his handwritten note to me:

> *I'll be with you in spirit, therefore I'll be with you. It's another hill for you, and the view will be wonderful . . . . You are privileged to be competing, so honor that privilege by your talent, your courage, your humility, and your compassion, and along with God's blessing and the ghosts of your kin, you will.*

These special words touched me deeply, and still do. Their message resonated with me that night, motivating me to do my absolute best. With them, the bonding between Jack Kendrick and me was cemented in a way that will last a lifetime. Jack has lived in Sweden for the last few years. The bonds established between us are so strong, we still talk at least once a week, over all that distance. One topic of conversation is always how my training is going. Jack is like a big brother to me. He is also one heck of a trainer and coach.

Ricky Young is a classic—a great boxer (pro record 18–4), a great motivator, and a terrific boxing trainer and corner man. Ricky has pushed me extremely hard in the five years or so we have worked together. He can speak to anyone about anything. He was as comfortable talking to Senator Bruno about politics and world events, as he is speaking with a man behind the counter at a drug store about the fights on a particular Saturday night. Early one Saturday morning, when a particular cab driver delayed us by driving to Gleason's in a roundabout, out-of-the-way route, making us late for a sparring session and annoying me, Ricky calmed the situation by dealing with the driver in soothing and problem-solving way. He is no-nonsense when he gives me advice, and I know better than to question or challenge anything he says. He has a great speaking voice, deep and resonating, and is comfortable addressing a large crowd. He is also very direct and forthright in working with me in those lonely moments between rounds in my corner.

Ricky and I are always trying new things together. He was thrilled when I began studying Bruce Lee, and we worked together to put Bruce Lee's teachings to good use. One of the words that he uses with me constantly is "relax." Through the teachings of Bruce Lee, I finally understood the meaning of that word. Ricky and I have used Bruce Lee's teachings to take my boxing to a higher level. The most valuable thing about Ricky Young is the positive attitude he has about everything, and that permeates every aspect in his life, and it's contagious. He's one of those people who lights up a room just by entering it.

I have been fortunate to have worked with Emanuel Steward, Jack Kendrick, Ricky Young, Pete Spanakos, Ron Johnson, Ronnie Cecchetti, and many other trainers from both Gleason's and the NYAC. They have made a huge difference in my ability to achieve my goals in the sport and be the best that I can be.

Jack Kendrick and Ricky Young are obviously special people, with unique backgrounds, as are all of the trainers I have used. What should *you* look for in a trainer? Who are these unsung heroes? What is their background? What do they charge for their services?

Most trainers are ex-professional boxers. Many were journeymen boxers, that is, professional boxers who go through all the hard training, always looking for their big break, but never rise high enough in the sport to make a good living. Professional boxing gyms are filled with these journeymen boxers, who work at the sport for many years but never make enough money to retire when their boxing career is over. Because of the rigor of the sport, retirement usually occurs when a boxer is in his mid-thirties, or at the latest in their early forties. So, after their career is done, many end up being trainers, or finding another career entirely. A trainer at Gleason's starts at about $25 for a one-hour training session, all of which they keep for themselves. There are periods during the day when trainers may not work, as there are peak and slack times when people come in during the day. There are no fringe benefits, no medical coverage, no retirement plan. It is fun to work in a boxing gym, but it's not a lucrative career.

For my money, I look for a trainer who can motivate me, and inspire confidence. I look for a connection, someone on the same wavelength as me, who understands me and the demands on my time, and inspires me to redouble my efforts to get in shape and stay in shape.

To properly convey the importance of a trainer to a boxer, let me share with you this story of professional boxing, which involves one of my heroes, the great Muhammad Ali. On February 25, 1964, Cassius Clay, as he was known in those days, got his shot at the Heavyweight Championship of the World. He was to fight the then-reigning champ Sonny Liston in Miami Beach, Florida. Liston was considered unbeatable by many, and was universally feared in the heavyweight division. As a heavyweight, Liston was from "central casting," as he was big, powerful and menacing in the ring, and threw bomb after unforgiving bomb. Nothing fazed him. Nevertheless, the young Cassius Clay had earned a shot at the title, and the stage had been set for the showdown.

Almost from the opening bell, the young Clay took control of the fight, and Sonny Liston was having trouble hitting him, particularly with his jab, which was one of the best in the business. Liston could lift people off the ground with his jab, but all it could find was air as Clay danced away from his reach. Liston had never seen anything like the superb footwork that Cassius Clay was demonstrating that night. Liston kept throwing big punches, most of them missing badly. Most others would be deflected as Clay cycled away. On the other hand, Clay was able to land some nice punches on Liston, gaining respect as the fight went on, and by the third round, Liston had a cut under his left eye. All was going well for Cassius through the first four rounds. Liston continued chasing Clay, swinging and missing. Clay's plan was to keep moving, tire him out, and then go on the attack. Clay was in complete control.

Towards the end of the fourth round, Clay's eyes began to sting. By the time the round ended and he was seated on the stool in his corner, the burning sensation increased and panic set in. As the pain grew worse, Clay was almost blinded. His trainer, Angelo Dundee, was to recount later, "Clay got something in his eyes. It was either from Sonny Liston's left eye, which was cut and had medication on it, or from Liston's shoulder, which was injured and had liniment on it." Clay was pawing at his face, fighting the pain in his eyes. He ordered Dundee to cut off his gloves. It was a tense moment. It would be the most important single minute of Dundee's career with Clay, which spanned decades and many championship fights. Without Dundee's instinctive reactions and cool-headedness at this precise moment, there might never have been a Muhammad Ali. Sonny Liston would have been unlikely to give a rematch to someone who humbled him, as Clay had done in the fight up until that point. Clay screamed at Dundee, wanting to quit. The pain was excruciating. More than perhaps any other time in his career, this was the moment of truth for the fighter who would one day become Muhammad Ali.

Dundee was cool and steady. "'This is the big one, daddy!' Dundee screamed in Clays' ear. 'Cut the bullshit. We're not quitting now.'" Dundee explained that he had seen this before, and Clay had to buy some time. Quickly he moved to take a sponge and get as much water into Clay's eyes as possible. Dundee told him to get out there and run, to "yardstick" him, meaning to keep moving and measuring him with his long left jab. Hopefully, this would give him enough time for the water to wash the substance out of his eyes. In those tense seconds, Dundee also had to deal with the Black Muslims who were sitting behind the corner. Between rounds, he had been informed that the Muslims were convinced that Dundee himself had blinded Clay on behalf of gangsters backing Liston. When the bell sounded for round five, Clay began to move slowly to the center of the ring, blinking madly. But he was on his feet, and still in the fight. Of course, if Clay had not trusted Dundee absolutely, things might have come apart in a hurry.

Liston went after Clay with everything he had. Clay could only open his eyes for seconds at a time, and then the pain was too great and he had to close them quickly. Liston was throwing hard shots at Clay, and connecting. Clay kept measuring him with his left hand, yardsticking him, and dancing away as best he could. Though Clay took some punishment, this strategy bought him the time he needed. With a half a minute left in the round, Clay's eyes cleared. From that moment on, there was no stopping Clay. Liston had won the fifth round, but the rest of the fight was all Clay. Liston did not answer the bell for the seventh round. Cassius Clay became the newly crowned Heavyweight Champion of the World.

Had Angelo Dundee not stood firm when Clay wanted to quit, Clay would have been disqualified and lost the fight. Admittedly, this is an extreme example of the importance of a trainer to a boxer in the outcome of a fight. However, boxing at any level of play is extremely fast moving, and there's little time to strategize. Trainers need to think on their feet instinctively. They are the only voice a boxer listens to during a fight, the only voice a boxer even hears.

Dundee sums up his feelings on his training methods thusly, "Training fighters . . . is like trying to catch a fish. It's technique, not strength. You got to play that fish nice and easy. And go with what's there. . . . You're not the same guy all the time. . . . You can't be an even-keel kind of guy. You gotta create things that are gonna help that fighter. And if it means gruffness and it means pushing him, and it means trying to put the bull on him, you gotta do it. Because the end result is you want to get that fighter juiced to try to win the fight. The name is winning. You gotta win." Of course, in white collar boxing, "winning" takes on a different context, because there is no winner or loser, per se. But as Bruce Silverglade has said many times, "Each fighter knows how things went on any particular night in the ring."

Dundee often said, "When I see things through my eyes, I see things." Though it's an oddball line, worthy of Yogi Berra, it's a perfect expression of Dundee's vision. Angelo Dundee lives, eats, and sleeps boxing. He was born to be in the corner of a boxing ring. He can spot the smallest flaw in a fighter's defense, such as the overextension of a right hand, or the slight dropping of the right hand when a fighter jabs with his left. The observance of these details, which might go unnoticed by most people, are invaluable to a fighter looking to penetrate the armor of an opponent. They can help a fighter win fights. When Angelo Dundee sees things through his eyes, he sees things. So does Ricky Young. So does Jack Kendrick.

A trainer also sees a fight from the best seat in the house, from the corner. He is almost inside the ring, in a position where he has a great vantage point. The fighter has a good position, too, but has the additional pressure of being engaged in the fight itself. The trainer has the advantage because he can see both fighters. He can look for flaws in both fighters, and pass all of this information on to his fighter between rounds.

However, it is also the job of the trainer to push the fighter to his limits, to challenge him or her in every possible way, to give credit for achievements but not at the expense of motivating the fighter to excellence. The demands placed on a fighter by a trainer can be very difficult at times, and the fighter has to have the utmost respect for his trainer to follow his every directive. The training can be grueling and harsh, like the fight itself. In a fight, the trainer often has to counter a fighter's natural, instinctive ability to merely survive, and simply persevere until the end of the fight. The trainer has to talk the fighter through tactics of how to win, how to demonstrate superior skills, and constantly remind him to do what's required to dominate an opponent. As Teddy Atlas said, "A trainer's got to lead a fighter into a dark place, and not too many want to go."

In the summer of 2004, I was to meet one of the greatest professional boxing trainers of all time. And we were destined to take a trip together later that year to the land where Broughton and Figg developed their skills. And, for me, it was to be the highlight of my boxing career, and an extremely rewarding journey.

CHAPTER 16

EMANUEL AND ME

One crowded hour of glorious life is worth an age without a name.
—COLONEL WILLIAM BARRETT TRAVIS, COMMANDER OF THE
TEXIAN ARMY AT THE ALAMO

Sometime in the early summer of 2004, I received a call from Alan Lacey of The Real Fight Club in London. Alan told me that he was helping organize a black tie charity night called Hedge Fund Fight Night, which was to be held on Wednesday, November 10, at the Marriott Hotel in Grosvenor Square in London. All of the participants were required to be active in the hedge fund industry, and he wanted me to fight a very senior, well-known industry executive at the event. It sounded like a great deal of fun, and a real challenge, so I jumped at the chance to participate.

No sooner had I hung up the phone with Alan Lacey, than I realized I'd committed to run the New York City Marathon on Sunday, November 7, in New York, and also to fight in Hedge Fund Fight Night on Wednesday, November 10, in London. I knew that was a tall order, physically, yet I really wanted to do both events. I asked people who had run marathons if they thought that taking part in both activities within a four-day period, on two different continents, was feasible. I made the same inquiry of various boxing trainers. The responses that came back were overwhelmingly negative. People urged me to make a decision as to which one I wanted to do. Because the opponent whom Alan Lacey had in mind for me had not yet committed to the fight on November 10, I decided to train for *both* the marathon and the fight, until I could tell for sure if I had a fight. I thought the cross training between boxing and running would be good for me, regardless of which event I chose. Thus began one of the most intense physical training periods of my life.

Then something totally unpredictable happened to me—I met Emanuel Steward. My friend, Rich Davemos, introduced us. Rich comes from a boxing family, and has invested in and worked with a few professional fighters. I had met Rich a few months earlier through my friend, and successful boxing trainer and manager, Tommy Gallagher, who recently had a starring role on *The Contender* television series.

Emanuel Steward can lay legitimate claim to being the greatest trainer and manager in boxing today. Over the course of his career in professional boxing, which began in 1969, he has trained and managed 31 world boxing champions, among them Lennox Lewis, Oscar De La Hoya, Evander Holyfield, Julio Cesar Chavez, and Tommy Hearns. Today, Emanuel is also a regular television commentator on HBO Sports and pay-per-view boxing events. A member of the International Boxing Hall of Fame since 1987, Emanuel is one of the most credible persons in the sport of boxing today and one of its true ambassadors. Emanuel is one of the most credible persons in the sport of boxing today. I was thrilled at the prospect of meeting him.

Emanuel came to town the next week, July 28, 2004, and we had dinner. I told him of my upcoming fight in London, and he asked me if he could train me for the fight and come to London with me to be in my corner. *He asked me!* You can tell me that you don't believe in Santa Claus, the tooth fairy, a pot of gold at the end of a rainbow, but I am here to tell you that magic sometimes does happen—or maybe it's just plain luck. Meeting Emanuel Steward was simply one of the most extraordinary things that has ever happened to me. Needless to say, I accepted his gracious offer without hesitation.

After spending the months of April, May, and June doing light sparring, combined with runs of about 15 miles a week, I began to accelerate my running in July. I decided to get my legs in shape first. I began running half marathons (over 13 miles), the furthest I had ever run up to that point in my career. I increased the distance I was running to 30 miles a week, during the months of July and August. In my marathon preparation, I did all of the "training runs," as supervised by the New York Road Runners Club, including one 20-mile run and two 18-mile runs, in addition to several half marathons and weekly organized runs of between four and six miles.

I was fortunate enough to attend the Olympics in Athens in August, where I spent half of my time in the boxing room. There I saw Teddy Atlas, who was doing the commentary for the American television stations. Teddy would sometimes give me his analysis of the fights after the daily session ended, which was great fun.

Teddy has a bit of a tough-guy, no-nonsense image. Not only was he a Golden Gloves champ, but he has a reputation of not being afraid to stand up to anyone who isn't treating him right, including Mike Tyson, who he used to train. In addition to being one of the best boxing trainers, analysts, and commentators in the sport, Teddy Atlas runs a foundation, named after his father (the Dr. Theodore A. Atlas Foundation), which has raised millions of dollars for all kinds of people in need. Teddy hosts a major black tie dinner in Staten Island each year, which has really put this foundation on the map and allowed it to gather sufficient funds to do a lot of good for a lot of people. After seeing Teddy at this dinner in November of 2004, and watching him interact with the crowd and the many, many people who the foundation has helped, I am convinced he has a heart of gold.

After returning from the Olympics in late August, I turned up the heat with my boxing training. By that time, my legs were in great shape because of the running I had been doing.

In the two months leading up to the fight, I had begun working out every Saturday morning with former #1 world heavyweight contender Gerry Cooney, who I had gotten to know through my involvement on the Board of Directors of a not-for-profit organization he founded in 1998, F.I.S.T. (Fighters' Initiative for Support and Training), which helps retiring boxers transition to another career. Gerry had heard about my fight in London and volunteered to help me. He showed me no mercy. In retrospect, I realize he was taking it easy on me, but it felt like he was throwing the kitchen sink at me. I have never been hit so hard before. I took everything he threw at me, learned a lot of great technique, and knew that I would not be facing anyone nearly as strong or as skilled as he. He gave me important instruction on keeping my punches short, throwing at least 20 jabs per round, controlling my breathing, and keeping my body positioned defensively at all times. It was also fun to work out with him at his private gym in New Jersey, a gym that Mike Tyson also uses. Gerry really helped me prepare for this fight, and I will be forever grateful. He spars 30 to 40 rounds per week to train aspiring boxers, most of which are junior high and high school students. He does this with no compensation or remuneration, but because he loves the sport, and loves helping people improve their skills and realize their potential. As he puts it, "I'm in better shape now, and know more about boxing, than when I fought for the heavyweight championship of the world."

I was really into a good boxing and running regimen in late September, when I checked in with Alan Lacey to see how things were shaping up for the November 10 fights. To my dismay, he said he was having trouble confirming that the man he had asked to be my opponent was going to fight. For some reason, he had decided to drop out. (I have always maintained that he "heard about me," as it was rumored that he had seen an article that described my boxing ability very favorably. But I really don't know what happened.) All I knew was that after all this time and preparation, all of sudden I was faced with the possible prospect of not fighting in the upcoming Hedge Fund Fight Night. At the same time, it bolstered my ego that my reputation as a boxer had apparently "crossed the pond."

Fortunately, a substitute opponent for me was arranged less than three weeks before the fight. At that point, I made the decision to take the fight in London, and forego the New York Marathon that year. I could run the marathon the following year. I phoned Emanuel to ask him if the offer to train me still stood, and he immediately agreed to come to New York to train me the week before the fight. There were still numerous obstacles to our training. Besides the difficulties of arranging the match itself (and the fact that the match was to be held in London), Emanuel lives in Detroit and I live in New York, and both of us travel constantly and have unpredictable demands on our time.

Emanuel Steward and the Kronk Gym in Detroit are synonymous with each other. They are both symbols of bigtime professional boxing. Emanuel started going to Kronk in the sixties, and really put it on the map. Indeed, Emanuel is justifiably credited with transforming Kronk from a neighborhood recreation center into one of the most famous boxing gyms in the world. Over the years, it has produced many amateur and professional boxing world champions, and is one of the most highly respected boxing gyms in the world today. Many of the greatest boxing champions of all time have trained there under Emanuel's tutelage.

Emanuel is a globetrotter, as a boxing commentator for HBO Sports, where he can be seen commentating on some of the biggest fights in boxing on a monthly basis. He is an excellent boxing analyst, trainer, and manager. He trains and/or manages many fighters, such as the Klitchko Brothers, Ronald Hearns (Tommy Hearn's son), and Vivian Harris, and is often seen in the corners in far off regions of the world. Emanuel is also one of the most credible people in the sport, and his opinions and analysis of fighters are highly regarded. For all of these reasons, I thought that it would be difficult, if not impossible, to actually pull this off. Nevertheless, when Lady Luck smiles at me, I always do my best to return the gesture.

We trained at the New York Athletic Club, in the club's boxing room. Emanuel loved the NYAC, and met many of my friends and teammates on the NYAC Boxing Team. We spent the entire week at the club working out together every day. I arranged a number of sparring partners from the NYAC Boxing Team, as well as from Gleason's Gym. As I live only one block from the NYAC, Emanuel and I were able to see each other frequently during the day, as well. I invited him over to see my collection of nineteenth-century boxing art, which he really enjoyed. In addition, we had dinner together almost every night. Emanuel visited my office in the Alliance Capital Building on Avenue of the Americas in New York, and admired the view of Central Park from the upper floors of the building.

On Thursday, November 4, 2004, Emanuel called me in a state of panic to tell me that his office reminded him that he'd committed to be at a black tie boxing fundraiser in Washington, D.C., on Thursday, November 11, the evening following Hedge Fund Fight Night. At this point, the cost of rebooking his ticket was prohibitively expensive. In one phone call, my office was able to arrange a decent ticket price for him, allowing him to attend both events. It was at this point we both began to realize that, despite the obstacles before us, there was something about this partnership that was meant to be.

The weekend before the fight, Emanuel had to go to Las Vegas to announce a fight for HBO, then returned to Detroit on Sunday, November 7, for a Monday evening departure to London. I left for London Monday morning, November 8, in preparation for the fight on November 10. Monday evening, November 8, Emanuel arrived at the Detroit airport one hour before his flight—without his passport! He had his office rush it to him, while authorities held the plane for 15 minutes. By rights, Emanuel should have missed that flight, which was the only daily direct flight from Detroit to London at that time. But once again we overcame huge obstacles and kept moving forward in pursuit of my dream.

Emanuel arrived in London Tuesday morning, November 9, and had some troubles with his hotel, which I was able to solve. He joined me on some of my business meetings in Mayfair. He told me he wasn't used to his fighters engaging in business activities before a fight, and enjoyed the experience. Tuesday night, Emanuel and I had a final workout at The Real Fight Club, and were joined by Alan Lacey. We were ready.

Wednesday, November 10, the day of the fight, Emanuel and I went to the office of Adrian Fairbourn, who is a director of Fund Advisors, a family office based in London. Hedge Fund Fight Night had been Adrian's brainchild. At Adrian's office, Emanuel and I were met by representatives of *BusinessWeek* magazine, which was preparing a story on white collar boxing. Then the afternoon was spent in mental preparation for the event that evening.

The night of the fight was a typical London one—cold and rainy. I went to Emanuel's hotel to pick him up. The event was black tie, so I had to carry my tuxedo with me, as I was only the second fight out on an eight-fight card. I was also carrying an enormous bag with all my boxing equipment. In my rush to pack for the trip, I had forgotten to bring my warm-up suit, so I was clad only in my boxing outfit—black shorts and a black Kronk Gym t-shirt with my name on the back in big bold, red letters. It was a gift Emanuel had presented to me in New York. When he saw me in the hotel lobby, he laughed that I was already prepared to jump in the ring. I wanted to laugh, too, but I was too busy freezing. Luckily we were able to get a cab to the Marriott Hotel in Grosvenor Square, only a short distance away.

We went straight to the second floor, where a few large suites had been reserved for the boxers' changing rooms. We were examined by a physician, as all the boxers were changing into their fight uniforms. All of the boxers except me had been issued uniforms—white tank tops and either blue or red silk shorts, depending on which corner they were in. For some reason, I had not gotten my uniform before the fight. No matter, I wanted to wear the Kronk boxing jersey that Emanuel had given me. I looked appropriately menacing—a bit like Darth Vader—which made me more confident. Emanuel changed into his own yellow Kronk t-shirt, which had in bold, red letters on the back "John Oden Training Camp." I was very honored to see Emanuel wearing that jersey. He taped my hands for me, tighter than any wrap I have experienced. I was taking great comfort from his being with me that night, and looking forward to having him in my corner.

The Real Fight Club puts on a very classy white collar boxing show. All of the fighters were marched into the ring, one by one, with *Rocky* music blaring, for the ceremonial weigh-in. It was in the lineup for this that I first spotted my opponent, Gray Smith. I had seen Gray's photo on the Internet, and recognized him instantly. He looked up at me, with no recognition. I leaned over and introduced myself, and mentioned to him that we would be meeting up later. Gray didn't say much, didn't smile at all. *Hmmm,* I thought to myself.

I weighed in at 14 stone, one pound. That converts to 197 pounds, the lightest I had weighed in a long time. I had really trained long, hard, and well for this fight. I had been told that my opponent, Gray Smith, was averaging 180 to 185 pounds. However, he weighed in at 14 stone, two pounds, one pound more than me. *Hmmm,* I thought again.

We went back to the dressing room, and Emanuel put on my headgear and gloves, and rubbed some Vaseline on my face. A fighter applies Vaseline to his face before a fight to give it a "slickness," so that punches will slide across the face rather than getting traction and "connecting" to the face. He grabbed a pair of my spare gloves to use as mitts to warm me up. Emanuel had instilled in me three things—keep my hands up, use straight punches, and don't drop my right hand when I jab. He had videotaped me at the NYAC, and showed me exactly what I was doing wrong. These lessons, and those that Gerry Cooney had drilled into me, proved to be invaluable once the contest began.

As the minutes ticked away, we went through a good warm-up, me punching the mitts, and Emanuel talking me through the drill. I was ready. I was really ready. I was actually looking forward to this match up. During this entire warm-up process, Emanuel was very cool, very calm, very professional. I was really glad he was with me.

We were told that it was time, and Emanuel and I began to make our way down the stairs, back into the grand ballroom, where the crowd was restless and excited. I heard the yelling and screaming from the first fight, which ended in a first-round knockout. I was motioned into the ring, sooner than I'd expected, and began the long walk towards it, with the theme from *Rocky* again blaring in the background. I felt good; I knew I had prepared well. I was nervous, but not at all panicked. It was natural to be nervous, even fearful. Fear is a powerful motivator in boxing. Fear is a boxer's friend. Over the years, I've come to understand its importance in the preparation for a fight.

I entered the ring first and moved around as Ricky Young

had taught me, getting a feel for the ring and the ropes. Gray entered the ring shortly after me.

The first introduction was Emanuel Steward, who was given a terrific introduction by the announcer. Among the 31 world champions Emanuel has trained was the great Lennox Lewis, who calls London home and had retired a year earlier as Heavyweight Champion of the World. I was introduced next, followed by Gray, who was 38 years old. I bowed to the crowd in all four directions, one of my trademarks over the years. The crowd, being predominantly British, was very partial to Gray, which was completely understandable, as it was his "home court." Emanuel and I went to the center of the ring, as did Gray and his trainer, Keith Wilson, a retired professional boxer, whom I had met on a previous trip to London. As the referee explained the rules, Gray looked very serious, very determined, frowning as the referee spoke. *Hmmm,* I thought for a third time.

We went back to our corners, the bell rang, and the fight began. Although Gray did not have a lot of ring experience, he was considered a good athlete and had trained hard for this fight. The age difference counted also, and Alan Lacey thought it would be a good match. He came out swinging with ruthless abandon. He was trying to knock me out fast. In the crowd was a friend of mine, John Allen, Chairman of Greater China Corporation, who later told me that everyone thought I was going to be knocked out in the first round, as Gray was really swinging at me. All they could see was Gray's elbows flying. What they could not see was that I was blocking or ducking every shot. He grazed me once or twice, but didn't really connect with anything. I paced myself, and unleashed a few jabs which kept him off balance. Emanuel had told me my jab was my best weapon, and that I should use it. I was doing my best to follow his advice.

The round ended, and I went back to my corner, where Emanuel had the stool waiting. I gladly sat down, awaiting

Emanuel's instruction. We had a pact before the fight that he would honestly tell me how I was doing between each round, and after the first round, help me with a game plan to adjust for the opponent in front of us. As I was sitting down, Emanuel said, "You won that round. You controlled the fight. You set the pace. He never really hit you." I said, "What now?" Emanuel said, "When he throws his big right hand, he overextends himself and exposes his right side. When that happens, hit him with your right." It was simple, straightforward, and exactly right! I got off my corner stool, and prepared myself for the next round.

The second round began quickly. Gray came at me harder. Then, in a flash, I watched him throw his right, really hard—overextending, then *POW,* I unleashed a short right hand that hit him flush in the eye and down he went on his back, hard. It all happened so quickly! I was so excited and discombobulated that I went over to my corner to see Emanuel, and the ref came running over to show me to a neutral corner. Gray got up, took the full count, and off we went again. The second round ended.

I went over to my corner and Emanuel said, "You won that round too!" He then said, "It's the last round, and he will come out really firing for the first 30 seconds. Let him punch himself out, and then hit him with your right again." Again, Emanuel's advice was simple, straightforward, and exactly on point. I looked out and saw a black eye forming on Gray, where I had hit him. I must admit that gave me additional confidence. I got off the stool, and waited for the final round to begin.

The bell rang and the third round began quickly. Sure enough, Gray was firing hard. I waited him out, and then hit him with a solid right hook. I had never thrown a right hook in my life! He went down again, this time on his face, hard. The ref waved both hands, indicating "fight over." Gray jumped up in protest. For some reason, the ref let the fight continue. However, most of the fireworks were over, and the fight ended soon enough. John Allen later told me that the crowd was ecstatic about the fight, and that I received a standing ovation. I was oblivious to all this, but it was very exciting. Gray and I embraced, and then I paid my respects to Keith Wilson, Gray's trainer.

I had brought two small flags with me, a U.S. flag and a Union Jack. I held them both up, one in each hand, and walked around the ring. With all the support that Great Britain has given us in the last few years, particularly in Iraq, and all the difficulties in the world today, I thought it was an appropriate gesture. It was well received. Gray and I met in the middle of the ring to receive our awards, and I gave him the Union Jack flag. The photographers went crazy; Gray even cracked a smile. Emanuel was beaming. I'm sure I was too. Much of the crowd was still on its feet. Alan Lacey was prancing around the ring like a proud panther. I didn't want to get out of the ring; it was so much fun. But the next fighters were standing by and it was time to go.

We went back to the locker room, amid cheers and well wishes from the other fighters. We showered up, put our tuxedos on, and wandered back into the grand ballroom, just in time to see Adrian Fairbourn working hard against a tough opponent. I ran into Gray Smith in the locker room and, later at the event, I walked over to say hello and wish him well. He was much friendlier now. We exchanged business cards and agreed to get in touch the next time our travels put us in the same city.

I was treated like a conquering hero. I met my friend, Alex Daly, who is with the brokerage firm, Man Financial, and we joined their table. Emanuel was introduced to everyone. People were awestruck when they realized who he was and all that he had accomplished in his life. I received congratulations from all. Emanuel insisted on phoning my sparring partner, Chris Angle, whom he had met the week before at the NYAC, to give him the good news. I placed a call to Gerry Cooney to relate the successful outcome, and he was very pleased.

We enjoyed the rest of the fights. Emanuel, however, was ecstatic. At one point later in the evening, he turned to me and said "You don't know what you did tonight. You executed perfectly. You did everything just the way I told you to. You have great credibility, because you knocked him down twice—that young guy! He came out swinging to take you out. If you hadn't kept to your strategy, it could have easily gone the other way. But, you followed *your* game plan. *You* controlled the action. This is a great experience for me—all of it, the NYAC, being with a professional businessman rather than a professional boxer, seeing your home, seeing your office in New York, attending your business meetings in London, watching the way you handle yourself, and being part of it. You should be very proud. I am so impressed. This was one of the greatest nights of my boxing career." As his comments began to sink in, I was truly prideful and thankful. Emanuel concluded his comments by saying, "John, tonight you orchestrated a beautiful symphony." I was speechless.

I think we said hello to everyone in the room—all four or five hundred of them. It was thrilling. John Allen asked us to join him for champagne at Annabel's, a traditional and very lively London night spot. We drank champagne and mused over the fight until the very early morning hours. Emanuel and John Allen had very early flights to the States the next morning, and I doubt if either of them slept at all.

The charity which benefited from Hedge Fund Fight Night was Operation Smile, an organization which provides reconstructive facial surgery to children and adults around the globe. The event netted £150,000 (approximately U.S. $270,000) to benefit Operation Smile. Interestingly, when the event was first proposed, the chairman of Operation Smile was not particularly keen on a boxing event as a fundraiser. He was persuaded by

Alan Lacey and others to give it a try. After seeing how the glamour and excitement of Hedge Fund Fight Night could work successfully to benefit his charity, he is most supportive of another such event in the future for Operation Smile.

A few days after I got back to New York, I received this email from Gray Smith, which I considered very classy and a terrific gesture of good sportsmanship:

> *Dear John,*
>
> *It was a great pleasure to meet you on Wednesday night. I have to say that I thoroughly enjoyed my first night of boxing and my first bout. You have kindly left me with a souvenir in the form of a very impressive black eye.*
>
> *As promised I am having the video of the bout copied and I will courier it to your office, hopefully during the course of next week.*
>
> *Next time you are in London, please do get in touch. I owe you a drink at the very least for the lesson you gave me in boxing, and I am sure you will be very welcome at the Fight Club gym sessions.*
>
> *And after all, I can tell my grandchildren that I was knocked over by one of Manny Steward's boxers.*
>
> *Kind regards,*
>
> *Gray Smith*

Since that time, Emanuel and I have had many great times together, reminiscing and celebrating the great night we had together. He has introduced me to his family—Emanuel travels to New York frequently. In early 2005, we attended *700 Sundays* together on Broadway, a one-man play starring Billy Crystal, a long-standing friend of Emanuel's.

Emanuel continues to tell the story of our London victory over and over again. Shortly after we got back to New York, he told me that it was one of the greatest nights he has ever spent in boxing, either as a boxer, trainer, manager, promoter, or broadcaster. He keeps a running list of his ten greatest nights in boxing, and my fight was number 7 on the list. Number 1 on the list is the night he won the National Golden Gloves Championship in the 118-pound division in 1963. He told me that nothing he has ever done or experienced in the ring, or outside of it, has equaled the exhilaration of this achievement.

In the rest of these fights, except mine, he acted as trainer and/or manager. Number 5 is the 1987 fight between Tommy Hearns and Juan Roldan, where Tommy became the first man in history to win world titles in four different weight classes. He was entered into the *Guinness Book of World Records* for this accomplishment. Tommy and Emanuel were invited to the White House to be honored by President Reagan following this victory.

Number 6 on the list, immediately preceding my fight, is the World Heavyweight Championship fight in June of 2002 between Lennox Lewis and Mike Tyson. Emanuel told me this was the biggest financial fight in history. It was an historic and emotional moment, as the "baddest man on the planet" was humbled so convincingly. This was a huge win for Lennox Lewis, as he dominated Tyson from the opening bell and knocked him out in the eighth round.

Number 9 on the list is the 1994 fight between Oliver McCall and Lennox Lewis. Oliver was a 10-1 underdog, and this was one of the biggest challenges of Emanuel's career. Emanuel and Oliver developed a specific plan, and Oliver scored a tremendous knockout over Lennox in the second round, becoming Heavyweight Champion of the World. After the fight, Lennox approached Emanuel to train him, and Emanuel accepted, because he believed in the long-term future of Lennox Lewis. However, in doing so, he had to give up Oliver, who was Heavyweight Champion of the World, and Julio Cesar Chavez, who was also a world champion and the hottest fighter in boxing at the time. Of course, as the history books will tell you, Lennox handily beat Oliver McCall in three rounds in their 1997 rematch, recapturing the World Boxing Council belt in the process. (The WBC is one of the sanctioning organizations in boxing. Their primary purpose is to rank the top fighters in each weight class.)

How did I, a white collar boxer, end up on Emanuel's list? I believe it was the uniqueness of the experience—the combination of things he had not dealt with before, coming together in a special way that inspired him. I am so different from anyone he had ever worked with before. I executed his strategy and instruction in a way that clearly pleased him and gave credibility to the effort by scoring two knockdowns. Through all this we had fun—training together at the NYAC, enjoying the boxing art in my apartment, attending my business meetings in London, being part of an impressive hedge fund event there. Part of it was that I took care of *him* to a certain extent, helping him sort out problems with his airline arrangements and hotel; generally the boxers he trains and manages look to him for everything. Both Emanuel and I tasted the sweet science that night—we both felt it all the way down to our socks! And it felt great. Given the limitations of my age, time requirements of my career, other responsibilities, combined with the Cinderella story of the way this fight came together and its outcome for me, I do not think it is an experience I will ever be able to top.

Emanuel and I are going to be friends for a long time. And the story of our great experience in London will be told again and again, for many years to come.

CHAPTER

17

THE ROAD
AHEAD

Success is never final.
—WINSTON CHURCHILL

So what's next? I feel great about everything that I've done in boxing. I'm in my fifties and work out at least three to five times a week, including some hard sparring, plus running and weights. I live a healthy life that's anything but boring. Due to the personal discipline I have developed because of my boxing for the past decade, I instinctively watch my diet and personal habits. I weighed under 200 pounds for my last fight in November 2004, which is a great weight for my 6'4" frame. There's a snap in my step that probably exceeds the one I had 20 years ago. I've gotten to know all these terrific people in the sport, many of whom are famous people.

The question is, was George Foreman's original premise right? At a certain age, does a man look ridiculous running down a road? Or lacing up a pair of boxing gloves? The older I get, the more I truly believe that a man can run down a road, or have a good boxing workout, at any age. By this, I don't mean I'm going to turn pro, or even box in white collar shows with any regularity, but a good workout—bag work, light sparring, jump rope, mitts, shadow boxing—can be done at any age. As to whether I have any other competitive matches, we'll see. I don't think I'll ever top what I did in London with Emanuel Steward. My mother always used to say, "Quit while you are ahead." There is wisdom in those words.

Of course, when you achieve success at anything, there's always someone who wants to challenge you. Alan Lacey says he has a billionaire he wants me to fight in London. There's a former pro at Gleason's who keeps telling me we should do a white collar boxing show. The NYAC boxing matches are always tempting. I completely relate to all the great champions who had trouble "hangin' 'em up" for good, like Ali, Foreman, Felix Trinidad, and Evander Holyfield. Even at the level of the sport at which I participate, the lure of the crowd and thrill of a good boxing challenge are really intoxicating. After all, how much fun will it be to say to people who continually ask me, "How's your boxing?"—to simply reply, "I'm retired." Despite all of the great experiences I have had in boxing, I think there will always be another challenge for me, looming just over the next horizon. The question becomes—which challenges will I answer?

Despite what I may do, or not do, in the ring, I have other ideas about how I can help the sport of boxing. I feel that I'm in a position to give something back to the sport. I have several ideas about how to do this. Because of my experience in white collar boxing, I have gotten to know a lot of people who are active in both professional and amateur boxing. There are probably numerous ways I could help the sport. The following three are definitely on my list.

International White Collar Boxing Association. In 2002 Alan Lacey of The Real Fight Club in London formed an organization called the International White Collar Boxing Association. It was established to determine a set of rules and guidelines for white collar boxing on a worldwide basis, an admittedly ambitious task. I was asked to serve on the Board of Directors, along with Bruce Silverglade, and my former opponent and English friend, Richard Williams. The Board to date has not been as active as one might expect. However, I love the idea of this bringing some worldwide order, and a set of rules and standards, to white collar boxing. Alan Lacey has recently promised to put forth his best efforts to do what he can to make it become an important governing body to this sub-set of the sport. As I mentioned, some feel that white collar boxing has become more important than professional boxing in London, and I think Alan could really make a contribution with this organization to the further development of white collar boxing worldwide. I am excited to be part of it.

Within the United States, white collar boxing is very fragmented, with Gleason's Gym still the mecca. There are many other boxing gyms where white collar boxers can be found, such as the Trinity Boxing Gym and Church Street Boxing Gym in New York, and the Wild Card Boxing Club in Hollywood, California. Emanuel Steward is interested in white collar boxing, and is looking into setting up a program in the famous Kronk Gym in Detroit. However, there is interest all over this country, including many smaller, lesser known gyms, and having some governing guidelines would be helpful. Alan regularly sees requests from groups in Australia, Russia, South Africa, Dubai, Canada, Germany and other parts of Europe, just to mention a random sampling. The way I see it—the more exposure the sport gets, the more people are going to understand it and embrace it. I have told Alan Lacey I will help him in any way to cement this organization and move it forward.

Fighters' Initiative for Support and Training (F.I.S.T.). Someone I have gotten to know over the last decade is Gerry Cooney. Since he retired from professional boxing, Gerry has become an ambassador to the sport of boxing.

In late 2003, Gerry Cooney asked me to join the Board of

Directors of a not-for-profit organization he formed in 1998, Fighters' Initiative for Support and Training (F.I.S.T.), which helps fighters transition from a boxing career to another career. There are volumes written about how many journeymen fighters get really used up in the ring, never make that much money, and then find themselves with no idea about how to support themselves when their skills decline and they can no longer fight well enough to earn a living. Many journeymen fighters make very low wages, and never build up enough money to have financial security. Gerry's foundation reaches out to organizations who can hire people, and he helps fighters find work. Largely through volunteer professionals whom he has recruited, he provides career and medical counseling to fighters who are retiring from the ring. F.I.S.T. has helped over 300 boxers make this transition.

In 2004, Gerry asked me to chair the first annual F.I.S.T. Fights for New York, a black tie boxing event which was attended by 650 people and raised money for over a dozen different New York based charities, including F.I.S.T., the Muscular Dystrophy Association, the Pediatric Cancer Foundation, the National Children's Leukemia Foundation, and the Lighthouse Foundation. I have been asked to chair Gerry Cooney's F.I.S.T. Fights for New York again this year, which will be held on October 26, 2005, and I have agreed to do so. I am proud to chair for a second year this major event for charity, which I think will help F.I.S.T. eventually become one of the most important, and influential, charities in all of sports.

New York City Public School Boxing at I.S. #174, Bronx, New York. Through my friends Pete and Nick Spanakos, I have become involved with the first-ever boxing program in the history of the New York City public school system, which is being offered at the Eugene T. Maleska Intermediate School #174 in the Bronx. The program is designed as an academically based fitness program, which stresses literacy and critical thinking through an environment of boxing training and academic scholarship. The program is open to students between the fifth and eighth grades. Professional educators work as coaches and tutors in the program, which is held from 3 to 6 o'clock three afternoons a week during the school year, plus a summer morning program. The program, centered around the sport of boxing, enables students to learn important academic skills by incorporating the sport as an area of academic study. Boxing classes are taught in conjunction with an academic class where students read and write articles, view films and discuss events, past and present, in boxing. The students' love of the sport keeps them focused and eager to participate in the boxing-related activities and instills a strong academic base. The program was developed by a very capable and enthusiastic counselor and social worker at the school, Matthew Ruggero. Matt, a Columbia University graduate with a master's degree in social work, now serves as the program's director.

Unfortunately, the local community, the infamous South Bronx section of New York City, is an economically depressed location. The area, known for its high crime rate and low per capita income level is a difficult environment for a child to grow up in. The students in the program are categorized under Title I as economically and educationally disadvantaged, and are drawn from the local housing projects in the area.

In 2004, F.I.S.T. named this school as one of the twelve beneficiaries from F.I.S.T. Fights for New York, and the money which the school received provided some of the initial funding of the boxing program. Because I was instrumental in making this happen, the school flattered me by naming a special program for "at-risk" fifth graders as "John E. Oden Boxing Scholars." This program is part of the "No Social Promotion Initiative" in New York Public Schools that mandates that students pass standardized reading and math exams before being advanced to higher grades, thereby ending the practice of "social promotion" whereby students matriculate to a higher grade based on age appropriateness rather than academic readiness. The initiative is currently in place at the third and fifth grade levels and is consistent with the tenets of President George W. Bush's "No Child Left Behind" educational reform legislation.

It should be noted that the entire boxing curriculum at the Eugene T. Maleska Intermediate School #174 is being watched with great interest in the other boroughs of New York City. Our long-term plan, based on the successful implementation of the programs at I.S. #174, is for these programs to spread throughout the entire public school system of New York City. An ulterior motive of mine is to be able to introduce boxing to students at a much earlier age than is currently practiced. After all, most schools have football teams, basketball teams, baseball teams, but no boxing team. If these efforts are successful, that could change.

These are three avenues which I am actively pursuing to help the sport of boxing, while doing good things for many people at the same time. White collar boxing has touched my life in more indelible ways than I could possibly mention. It is hard for me to gauge in what direction I will apply my energies from here, or what paths I will take. One thing is for sure, though. Whether I am in or out of the ring, I'll be swinging harder than ever.

John Oden, left, pals around with Gerry Cooney.

Boxing Record of John Oden

DATE & TRAINER	OPPONENT, PROFESSION, & GYM	WON/LOST	LOCATION & COMMENTS
10/25/1993 Ronnie Cecchetti	Scott "Slick" Butler, investment banker, former partner at Drexel Burnham, NYAC	Won	Location—NYAC. 125th NYAC Championships. Only heavyweight fight of the night.
4/19/1995 Ronnie Cecchetti	John "The Torturer" Turco, electrical contractor, owner of A.J. Electric, Chairman of the Boxing Team of the Downtown Athletic Club	Draw	Location—NYAC. NYAC–DAC challenge match. I was robbed. Knocked him down in the third round. Fight ended when he was flat on his back—I think they rang the bell early.
10/18/1995 Ronnie Cecchetti	John "The Torturer" Turco	Lost	Location—DAC. NYAC–DAC challenge match. Training disrupted because of a death in my family. Decided to honor commitment to fight anyway. As a result, I performed below my potential.
10/23/1996 Ronnie Cecchetti & Jack Kendrick	John "The Torturer" Turco	Draw	Location—DAC. NYAC–DAC challenge match. Turco tackled me twice in the first round. Otherwise, a good, even match.
11/21/1997 Darius Ford	Bill Logan, writer, Gleason's Gym	White collar sparring	Location—Gleason's. Think I won this one.

Boxing Record of John Oden

Date & Trainer	Opponent, Profession, & Gym	Won/Lost	Location & Comments
6/11/1999 Ron Johnson	Craig Toomen, architect, Gleason's Gym	White collar sparring	Location—Gleason's. I hit him hard in the second round. However, he came out firing in the third, and gave me a bloody lip. Think I might have gotten the decision, but close, maybe a draw.
5/11/2000 Ron Johnson	Mark Settembre, real estate developer, NYAC	Won	Location—NYAC. NYAC championships. One of only two heavyweight fights.
6/2/2000 Ron Johnson	Mark Settembre	White collar sparring	Location—Gleason's. Much closer fight. Pretty even.
7/13/2000 Ricky Young	Dr. Marcus Overhaus, derivatives trader, Deutsche Bank, The Real Fight Club —London	White collar sparring	Location—Broadgate Arena in London, an open air arena in the financial district. Easy win.

Boxing Record of John Oden

DATE & TRAINER	OPPONENT, PROFESSION, & GYM	WON/LOST	LOCATION & COMMENTS
7/28/2000 Ricky Young	Chris "Whiplash" Angle, commodities investment advisor, Asset/Risk Management, NYAC	White collar sparring	Location—Gleason's. My regular sparring partner, Chris Angle, agreed to a Gleason's match in connection with a documentary film being made. Jack Kendrick said it was my night.
11/17/2000 Ricky Young & Jack Kendrick	Richard Williams, librarian, London & Quandrant Housing Trust, The Real Fight Club —London	White collar sparring	Location—Gleason's. A U.S. versus London challenge match. I knocked Richard down in the first round to coast to an easy victory.
6/14/2001 Ricky Young	Lee Victory, bond trader, Cantor Fitzgerald, The Real Fight Club—London	White collar sparring	Location—Royal National Hotel in Russell Square in London. A black tie U.S. versus London challenge match benefiting charity. One of the toughest fights I have ever had. Jack Kendrick said I took it, but I would have been happy with a draw.

Boxing Record of John Oden

DATE & TRAINER	OPPONENT, PROFESSION, & GYM	WON/LOST	LOCATION & COMMENTS
10/19/2001 Ricky Young	Perry D'Alessio, CPA, D'Alessio & Associates, Gleason's Gym	White collar sparring	Location—Gleason's Gym. MSNBC made a one-hour television special about the fights. Jack Kendrick said I got the nod, but we both fought well.
8/22/2002 Ricky Young	Chris "Whiplash" Angle	White collar sparring	Location—NYAC. This was a NYAC boxing team exhibition. Chris Angle had sore ribs, and I agreed not to hit him in the midsection, which cramped my style. Probably a boring fight, as I was limited in what I could do, and we clinched often because I could not bang away at him.
10/10/2002 Ricky Young	Detective Dave Melin, undercover policeman, head of the "gang squad" in Staten Island, NYPD	Lost	Location—NYAC. Bouts between the NYAC and NYPD. Very close match, with a number of people surprised that the decision went against me.

Boxing Record of John Oden

Date & Trainer	Opponent, Profession, & Gym	Won/Lost	Location & Comments
10/18/2003 Matthew Said Muhammad	Pat O'Lear, fireman, Detroit Fire Department	White collar sparring	Location—Gleason's Gym boxing camp in the Catskills. Even though Mr. O'Lear outweighed me by 50 pounds, I coasted to an easy win.
11/21/2003 Ricky Young	Dave Berman, undergraduate student at Columbia University	White collar sparring	Location—Gleason's Gym. Opponent was 19 years old, and a member of the Columbia University Boxing Team. Didn't lay a glove on me. This was among my best nights ever as a student of the sweet science.
11/10/2004 Emanuel Steward & Gerry Cooney	Gray Smith, hedge fund attorney, Maples and Calder, The Real Fight Club —London	White collar sparring	Location—Marriott Hotel in Grosvenor Square in London. A black tie charity fundraiser. Gerry Cooney had trained me for two months leading up to the fight. With Emanuel Steward in my corner, I knocked Gray down in both the second and third rounds to coast to my personal best and a standing ovation from the British crowd.

RESOURCES

Books

Hatmaker, Mark, with Doug Werner. *Boxing Mastery.* San Diego, California: Tracks Publishing, 2004.

Onello, R. Michael. *Boxing: The American Martial Art, A 12-Week Boxing Course.* Hartford: Turtle Press, 2003.

Scott, Danna. *Boxing: The Complete Guide to Training and Fitness.* New York: The Berkley Publishing Group, a division of Penguin Group, 1999.

Todd, Gary. *Workouts From Boxing's Greatest Champs.* Berkeley, California: Ulysses Press, 2005.

Werner, Doug. *Boxer's Start-Up: A Beginner's Guide to Boxing.* San Diego, California: Tracks Publishing, 1998.

Videos & DVD's

Attacking and Punching at Angles—Keep Your Opponent on the Defensive. Title Boxing, 2003.

Boxing Defensive Skills and Drills—Hit and Don't Get Hit. Title Boxing, 2003.

How to Box—The Basics. Title Boxing, 2003.

How to Hit the Heavy Bag. Title Boxing, 2003.

Jennings, Joe. *Ultimate Boxing Fundamentals.* Topboxing.com, 2003.

Olajide, Michael Jr. *Everlast Boxing Workout: Beginner.* Everlast, 2004.

Olajide, Michael Jr. *Everlast Boxing Workout: Advanced.* Everlast, 2004.

Weldon, Kenny. *Learn To Box, Vols. 1-4.* Neutral Corner Media, 1994.

Websites

www.boxingscene.com

www.encyclopedia.thefreedictionary.com/boxing

www.everlastboxing.com

www.gleasonsgym.net

www.JohnEOden.com

www.ringside.com

www.therealfightclub.co.uk

www.titleboxing.com

www.usaboxing.org

Gyms & Clubs

Atlanta Art of Boxing Center
1135 Spring Street
Atlanta, GA 30309
Ph: 404-870-8444
www.artofboxing.net

Boston Sport Boxing Club
125 Walnut Street
Watertown, MA 02472
Ph: 617-972-1711
www.bostonboxing.com

Church Street Boxing Gym
25 Park Place
New York, NY 10007
Ph: 212-571-1333
www.nyboxinggym.com

Fitplex
1235 N LaSalle
Chicago, IL 60610
Ph: 312-640-1235
www.fitnessformulaclubs.com

Gleason's Gym
83 Front Street
Brooklyn, New York
Ph: 718-797-2872
www.gleasonsgym.net

Gold Coast Gym
1235 North LaSalle
Chicago, IL 60610
Ph: 312-640-1235
www.goldcoastboxing.com

Hamlin Park Boxing Club
3034 North Hoyne
Chicago, IL 60618
Ph: 312-742-7785

Harrowgate Boxing Club
1920 E Venango Street
Philadelphia, PA 19134
Ph: 215-744-5503

JABB Boxing Gym
410 N Oakley, 2nd Floor
Chicago, IL 60612
Ph: 312-733-JABB (5222)
www.jabbboxing.com

Knock-Out Boxing Club
10355 Hammocks Boulevard, 2nd Floor
Miami, FL 33196
Ph: 305-388-1129
www.knockoutboxingclub.com

Kronk Gym
5555 McGraw Street
Detroit, Michigan 48225
Ph: 313-894-0796
www.kronkgym.com

Langton Boxing & Martial Arts
1006 W Oak Street
Burbank, CA 91506
Ph: 323-461-4170
www.langtonboxing.com

The Real Fight Club
3 Tudor Street
London EC4Y OAH
England
Ph: 44-7903-442-4552
www.therealfightclub.co.uk

South Florida Boxing
715 Washington Avenue
Miami Beach, FL 33139
Ph: 305-672-8262
www.southfloridaboxinggym.com

The Trinity Boxing Club
110 Greenwich Street
New York, NY 10006
Ph: 212-374-9393
www.trinityboxing.com

Wild Card Boxing Club
1123 Vine Street
Los Angeles, CA 90038
Ph: 323-461-4170

The World Gym
16 Sturtevant Street
Somerville, MA 02145
Ph: 617-628-4272

NOTES

CHAPTER 2. THE SWEET SCIENCE

Page 16: " '. . . of grace and beauty.' " Gorn, Elliott J. *The Manly Art.* Ithica, New York: Cornell University Press, 1986, p. 22.

Page 17: " '. . . gleaming with oil.' " Carpenter, Harry. *Boxing, an Illustrated History.* London: Crescent Books, a division of Crown Publishers, Inc., 1975 first printing, first English edition published by William Collins in 1975, updated in 1982, p. 10.

Page 19: " '. . . part of the attraction.' " Egan, Pierce. *Boxiana.* London: The Folio Society, 1976, a selection, edited and introduced by John Ford, p. 6.

Page 20: " '. . . art for gentlemen.' " Seltzer, Robert. *Inside Boxing.* New York: Michael Friedman Publishing Group, 2000, p. 19.

Page 20: " '. . . opponents beyond measure.' " Egan, Pierce. *Boxiana.* London: The Folio Society, 1976, a selection, edited and introduced by John Ford, p. 24.

Page 21: " '. . . animated and cheerful.' " Egan, Pierce. *Boxiana.* London: The Folio Society, 1976, a selection, edited and introduced by John Ford, p. 29.

Page 22: " '. . . crude slugger.' " Fleischer, Nat, and Sam E. Andre. *A Pictorial History of Boxing.* New York, New: A Citadel Press Book. Published by Carol Publishing Group. Originally published, 1959. Revised and updated, 1993, pp. 18–20.

Page 24: " '. . . moment and motion.' " Gorn, Elliott J. *The Manly Art.* Ithica, New York: Cornell University Press, 1986, pp. 201–202.

Page 29: " '. . . Poetry in motion?' " Seltzer, Robert. *Inside Boxing.* New York: Michael Friedman Publishing Group, 2000, p. 9.

Page 30: " '. . . but Robinson could.' " Seltzer, Robert. *Inside Boxing.* New York: Michael Friedman Publishing Group, 2000, p. 39.

Page 31: " '. . . is of one piece.' " Liebling, A.J. *The Sweet Science.* London: The Sportsmans Book Club, 1958, pp. 110–112.

Page 32: " '. . . and a rugged handsomeness.' " Liebling, A.J. *The Sweet Science.* London: The Sportsmans Book Club, 1958, p. 109.

CHAPTER 5. MY FIRST FIGHT NIGHTS

Page 60: ". . . referred to as 'a reach.' " McDermott, Jack. "Sports Review—Boxing." The Magazine of the New York Athletic Club, *The Winged Foot,* November 1993, p. 54.

Page 64: " '. . . was called a draw.' " Cecchetti, Ron. "Club
Sports Review—Boxing." The Magazine of the New York
Athletic Club, *The Winged Foot*, August 1995, p. 55.

CHAPTER 6. GLEASON'S GYM

Page 84: ". . . more muscular foe." Foxen, Dave. "Boxing
Battles Back." The Magazine of the New York Athletic
Club, *The Winged Foot*, July 2000, pp. 21–22.

CHAPTER 7. LONDON CALLING

Page 87: " '. . . have an agenda.' " Moss, Stephen. "Glove
Story." *The Guardian*, May 2, 2000.

Page 93: ". . . world for centuries." Spanakos, Dr. Nikos
Michalis. "An Evening Today at Gleason's." *Brooklyn
Heights Press & Cobble Hill News*, November 30, 2000.

Page 94: ". . . fantasies come true." Rubin, Courtney. "The
Lords of the Ring." *Time*, September 22, 2003, p. 65.

Page 95: "Don't watch!" www.therealfightclub.co.uk

CHAPTER 10. FIGHTING COPS, FIREMEN, SENATORS, AND HILARY SWANK

Page 124: ". . . exchanges and the decision." Harden, Doug.
"The New York Athletic Club/Heroes Battle for the
Prize." *Spitbucket News*, October 10, 2002.

Page 125: ". . . was declared the winner." Ryan, Tom. "Fortune
Favors the Brave." The Magazine of the New York Athletic
Club, *The Winged Foot*, December 2002, p. 27.

Page 130: "... to come back naturally." Hoffman, Jascha. "A Couple of Heavyweights." *New York Sun,* October 22, 2003. John Oden is a Principal on the money management side of Bernstein Investment Research and Management, part of Alliance Capital.

CHAPTER 12. "FARANG BA"

Page 151: " '... or not, ultimately doesn't matter.' " Sullivan, John. *Farang Ba (Crazy White Foreigner).* USA/Thailand: Naked Emporer Productions, 2002.

CHAPTER 13. THE INCOMPARABLE, UNCONQUERABLE BRUCE LEE

Page 156: " '... go through his paces.' " Editors of "Black Belt Magazine." *The Legendary Bruce Lee.* Santa Clarita, California: Ohara Publications, 1986, p. 106.

Page 156: " '... the soulsearcher.' " Little, John. *Bruce Lee: Artist of Life.* Boston: Tuttle Publishing, 1999, p. xiv.

Page 157: " '... I met a rival gang.' " Editors of "Black Belt Magazine." *The Legendary Bruce Lee.* Santa Clarita, California: Ohara Publications, 1986, p. 10.

Page 159: "... (the Tao) of Ali," Miller, Davis. *The Tao of Bruce Lee.* London, England: Vintage, 2000, p. 105.

Page 160: " '... discover for himself.' " Editors of "Black Belt Magazine." *The Legendary Bruce Lee.* Santa Clarita, California: Ohara Publications, 1986, p. 69.

Page 161: " '... 50-year-old man alive.' " Uyehara, M. *Bruce Lee: The Incomparable Fighter.* Santa Clara, California:

Ohara Publications, p. 65.

Page 163: " '. . . fit into any container.' " *and* page 163:
" '. . . the nature of water.' "Cohen, Rob and Ed
Khmara, screenplay. Produced by Rafella de Laurentus.
Dragon: The Bruce Lee Story. Universal City Studios, 1993.

Page 163: " '. . . punch or hurt it' " *and* page 164: " '. . . Be
water, my friend.' " Little, John. *A Warrior's Journey*. JJL
Enterprises, A John Little Film, 2000.

Page 164: " '. . . its destiny sure.' " Lee, Bruce. Edited by John
Little. *Striking Thoughts: Bruce Lee's Wisdom for Daily
Living*. Boston: Tuttle Publishing, 2000, p. 108.

Page 164: " '. . . like a hot summer's day.' " Little, John. *Bruce
Lee: Artist of Life*. Boston: Tuttle Publishing, 1999, p. 9.

Page 164: " '. . . got to keep on flowing.' " Little, John. *Bruce
Lee In His Own Words: Commentaries on the Martial Way*. A
John Little Production, 1998.

Page 165: " '. . . of the universe.' " Little, John. *Bruce Lee: Artist
of Life*. Boston: Tuttle Publishing, 1999, p. 3.

Page 165: " '. . . the principle of growth.' " L. Frank N.
Magill. *Masterpieces of World Philosophy, New York*: Harper
Collins Publishers, 1990, p. 111.

Page 169: " '. . . always strangely purifying.' " Miller, Davis.
The Tao of Bruce Lee. London, England: Vintage, 2000,
p. 5.

CHAPTER 15. IN MY CORNER

Page 181: "... does not massage the pitcher." Remnick,
David. "Cornerman: Teddy Atlas and the Art of
Bruising." *The New Yorker,* August 21 & 28, 2000, p. 147.

Page 182: "...on top of the world." and page 182: "... like we
are family." Sullivan, John. *Farang Ba (Crazy White Foreigner).*
USA/Thailand: Naked Emporer Productions, 2002.

Page 186: " '... had liniment on it.' " Fried, Ronald K.
Corner Men: Great Boxing Trainers. New York: Four Walls
Eight Windows, 1991, p. 4.

Page 186: " ' "... not quitting now." ' " Remnick, David.
King of the World. New York: Random House, 1998,
p. 196.

Page 188: " '... You gotta win.' " Fried, Ronald K. *Corner
Men: Great Boxing Trainers.* New York: Four Walls Eight
Windows, 1991, pp. 9–10.

Page 188: " '... through my eyes, I see things.' " Fried,
Ronald K. *Corner Men: Great Boxing Trainers.* New York:
Four Wall Eight Windows, 1991, p. 28.

Page 189: " '... not too many want to go.' " Remnick,
David. "Cornerman: Teddy Atlas and the Art of
Bruising." *The New Yorker,* August 21 & 28, 2000, p. 153.

SELECTED BIBLIOGRAPHY

BOOKS

Carpenter, Harry. *Boxing, an Illustrated History.* London: Crescent Books, a division of Crown Publishers, 1975 first printing, first English edition published by William Collins in 1975, updated in 1982.

Christopoulos, George A. and John C. Bastias. *The Olympic Games in Ancient Greece.* Athens, Greece: Ekdotike Athenon S.A., 1982.

Egan, Pierce. *Boxiana.* London: The Folio Society, 1976, a selection, edited and introduced by John Ford.

Editors of "Black Belt Magazine." *The Legendary Bruce Lee.* Santa Clarita, California: Ohara Publications, Inc., 1986.

Fleischer, Nat, and Sam E. Andre. *A Pictorial History of Boxing.* New York, New: A Citadel Press Book. Published by Carol Publishing Group. Originally published, 1959. Revised and updated, 1993.

Fried, Ronald K. *Corner Men: Great Boxing Trainers.* New York: Four Walls Eight Windows, 1991

Golden, Mark. *Sport in the Ancient World From A to Z.* London: Routledge Taylor & Francis Group, 2004.

Gorn, Elliott J. *The Manly Art*. Ithica, New York: Cornell University Press, 1986

Lee, Bruce. Edited by John Little. *Striking Thoughts: Bruce Lee's Wisdom for Daily Living*. Boston: Tuttle Publishing, 2000.

Liebling, A.J. *The Sweet Science*. London: The Sportsmans Book Club, 1958.

Little, John. *Bruce Lee: Artist of Life*. Boston: Tuttle Publishing, 1999.

Little, John. *Bruce Lee: Jeet Kune Do*. Boston: Charles E. Tuttle Co., 1997.

Mee, Bob. *Boxing: Heroes & Champions*. Edison, New Jersey: Chartwell Books, 1997.

Miller, Davis. *The Tao of Bruce Lee*. London, England: Vintage, 2000.

Miller, Davis. *The Zen of Muhammad Ali*. London, England: Vintage, 2002.

O'Brien, Richard. *The Boxing Companion*. New York: A Friedman Group Book publishes by the Mallard Press, an imprint of BDD Promotional Book Company, 1991.

O'Reilly, John Boyle. *The Ethics of Boxing and Many Sports*. Boston, 1888, chapters 13, 15.

Remnick, David. *King of the World*. New York: Random House, 1998.

Seltzer, Robert. *Inside Boxing*. New York: Michael Friedman Publishing Group, 2000

Sugar, Bert. *Bert Sugar On Boxing*. Guilford, Connecticut: The Lyons Press, 2003.

Sun-Tzu. *The Art of War*. Barnes & Noble Books, by arrangement with Westview Press. Translated by Ralph D. Sawyer, 1994.

Thomas, Bruce. *Bruce Lee: Fighting Spirit*. Berkeley, California: Frog, 1994.

Uyehara, M. *Bruce Lee: The Incomparable Fighter*. Santa Clara, California: Ohara Publications.

PUBLICATIONS AND NEWSPAPER ARTICLES

Cecchetti, Ron. "Club Sports Review—Boxing." The Magazine of the New York Athletic Club, *The Winged Foot*, August 1995.

Foxen, Dave. "Boxing Battles Back." The Magazine of the New York Athletic Club, *The Winged Foot*, July 2000.

Harden, Doug. "The New York Athletic Club/Heroes battle for the Prize." *Spitbucket News*, October 10, 2002.

Hoffman, Jascha. "A Couple of Heavyweights." *New York Sun*, October 22, 2003.

Lence, Rudy. "The History of NYAC Boxing." The Magazine of the New York Athletic Club, *The Winged Foot*, February 2003.

McDermott, Jack. "Sports Review—Boxing." The Magazine of the New York Athletic Club, *The Winged Foot,* November 1993.

Moss, Stephen. "Glove Story." *The Guardian,* May 2, 2000.

People. "50 Most Beautiful People." May 10, 2004.

Remnick, David. "Cornerman: Teddy Atlas and the Art of Bruising." *The New Yorker,* August 21 & 28, 2000.

Rubin, Courtney. "The Lords of the Ring." *Time,* September 22, 2003.

Ryan, Tom. "Fortune Favors the Brave." The Magazine of the New York Athletic Club, *The Winged Foot,* December 2002.

Spanakos, Dr. Nikos Michalis. "An Evening Today at Gleason's." *Brroklyn Heights Press & Cobble Hill News,* November 30, 2000.

Stout, David. "Stepping Into the Ring and Stepping into Character." *The New York Times,* May 15, 1996.

Van Biema, David. Reported by Susanne Lingemann. 'The Gym." *Time,* 1986.

Wexler, Sanford. "Wall Street Heavyweights." *Trader's Magazine,* September 2000.

FILMS

Bailey, Joanna. *The Pain Business.* Optomen Television, Channel 4 Television, London, 2000.

Cohen, Rob and Ed Khmara, screenplay. Produced by Rafella de Laurentus. *Dragon: The Bruce Lee Story.* Universal City Studios, 1993.

A Cort/Madden Production, *Against the Ropes,* Paramount Pictures, in association with MMP Erste Film Productions, GMBH, 2003.

Little, John. *Bruce Lee in His Own Words: Commentaries on the Martial Way.* A John Little Production, 1998.

Little, John. *A Warrior's Journey.* JJL Enterprises, A John Little Film, 2000.

Sullivan, John. *Farang Ba (Crazy White Foreigner).* USA/Thailand: Naked Emporer Productions, 2002.

Weintraub, Fred, and Paul Heller. *Enter the Dragon, Special 25th Anniversary Edition.* : Warner Brothers, 1998, based on original film, 1973.

Wilson/Golding Productions. *MSNBC Investigates Fight Night.* New York: MSNBC, 2001.

WEBSITES

www.encyclopedia.thefreedictionary.com/boxing

www.everlastboxing.com

www.gleasonsgym.net

www.ringside.com

www.therealfightclub.co.uk

www.titleboxing.com

www.usaboxing.org

With special thanks
and great appreciation to:

Darcy L. Reed